IDENTIFYING
METALLIC SMALL FINDS

Anglia Publishing
Watts House
Capel St. Mary, Ipswich
Suffolk, IP9 2JB

First published in Great Britain by the author, 1992.
Published by Anglia Publishing, Ipswich, 1994.
2nd revised edition published by Anglia Publishing, Ipswich, 1993.

© M. J. Cuddeford, 1994.

Printed in Great Britain by Suffolk Offset, Martlesham, Suffolk.

ISBN: 1 897874 09 X. 2nd revised edition.
(ISBN: 1 897874 04 9. 1st edition).

CONTENTS

	Page
Foreword	1
Ammunition	3
Bells	4
Bronze Age Artefacts	5
Buckles	8
Buttons	15
Clasps and Fasteners	20
Horseshoes	22
Jewellery	24
Keys	31
Mounts and Fittings	33
Seals and Seal Boxes	42
Spoons	45
Thimbles	48
Weights	49
Miscellaneous	51
Select Bibliography	60

FOREWORD

This booklet is intended to assist in the identification of metallic small finds, and it is hoped that it will be of use to anyone who has need of a general reference source. Whether archaeologist, museum curator, metal detector user or antiquity collector, identifying small finds often involves referring to scattered articles in publications, or excavation reports which invariably contain a great deal of architectural and ceramic data in addition to often brief selections of small finds.

Deciding what to illustrate presents an immediate problem, as the range of possible items and fragments of items is almost limitless, and whereas some things are easily categorised by type or function, many are not. However, it is simpler to decide if a find is some kind of decorative mount or a brooch than to try and decide to which period it belongs, and thus it is easier to refer to the probable category. It must be appreciated that in a general work of this size, the following illustrations are typical of many common finds, but still leave a vast body of material and variation uncovered. With many things, it will be necessary to consult more comprehensive books dealing with particular types of object in order to obtain closer comparisons with finds.

When finds are random and unstratified, dating cannot be based on associated material alone. There is certainly a strong possibility that an item from a Roman site may well be Roman in date, but also a very good chance of it being medieval or recent as well, and so caution must always be exercised when trying to date or attribute uncertain or fragmentary objects which are not proven from archaeological or typological study. Most of the following objects illustrated have been ascribed a function, but this is on occasion the result of educated guesses, rather than concrete factual evidence, and so the opportunity always exists for someone to solve a mystery or change opinions. It used to be a standard joke in archaeological circles that anything that did not appear to have an obvious function was described as a 'ritual' object. We tend now to credit the Ancients with some sense of trivia - in other words a statue of a god probably did stand in the family shrine, but a bronze model of a dog probably sat on the mantlepiece for no other reason than it was decorative. In the same way it is often impossible to be too pedantic when deciding what some of the items illustrated in the following pages were actually used for and how they were regarded. A great number of decorative fixings occur that we describe as harness trappings, but some were possibly items of personal adornment or affixed to furniture; unless we have an original item or illustration with such things in situ, we can only make guesses based on the method of attachment and find distribution etc.

Many objects are easily identifiable with their particular period, and often display a remarkable continuity of conservativeness. Artefacts such as Bronze Age axes and early Roman brooches rarely vary in decoration or typological form despite the opportunity for elaboration. Some practical items like certain tools hardly change at all, and a Roman iron hammer may look much the same as a recent one. Elsewhere there is considerable variety, later Roman brooches and Tudor buckles being a good example. Although categorisable as 'plate brooch' or 'spectacle buckle', the imagination of the individual makers allowed for a wide range of design detail, and for this reason it is never possible to illustrate the many variations to be found, with new ones occuring all the time. Because of this, it must always be borne in mind that in trying to identify a find using the following pages, an exact match will rarely occur, and it will be the general form together with certain characteristics that in most cases allow an item to be identified. It is of the utmost importance to recognise the component parts of certain things which will often occur as separate fragments in the field, and I have illustrated a number of fragmentary items that are often encountered as well as depicting the complete objects themselves. Only a few iron objects are included due to their generally poor survival rate in non-anaerobic contexts, and those included have been limited to a small range of finds that are quite frequently recovered and are readily identifiable. All objects illustrated are therefore copper-alloy unless otherwise stated.

The periods to which this volume refers are somewhat arbitrary, and follow convention rather than precise phases and dates. Invasion dates such as 43 AD or 1066 are meaningless as far as many artefacts are concerned, and there is considerable overlap with certain styles of object spanning two if not three periods. 1820 is a convenient date to regard as 'recent,' as mass production began to create such a wide diversity of design difference in many things that it would not be possible to cover them all.

Periods;			
Bronze Age	c2300	-	700 BC
Iron Age	c700 BC	-	50 AD
Roman	c50	-	400 AD
Saxon	c400	-	1100 AD
Medieval	c1100	-	1500 AD
Tudor	c1500	-	1600 AD
Stuart	c1600	-	1700
Georgian	c1700	-	1820 AD
Recent	c1820	-	Present.

SCALE: All illustrations are depicted actual size unless otherwise stated in the text.

AMMUNITION

Early musket balls rarely conformed to an exact calibre, and a bullet mould was usually provided to match the bore of each individual gun. Calibre is expressed as fractions of an inch or in millimetres, or by how many balls per pound of lead could be produced, and thus 12 bore is 12 balls to the pound.

1. This medium size ball dates from the civil war period.

2. A large ball from a 'Brown Bess' musket of the Napoleonic period.

3. This small calibre ball is typical of the many flintlock and percussion weapons widely owned by civilians in the 18th and 19th centuries. Bores became standardised, with .36 and .44 popular for revolvers of military type. Early revolvers such as Colts and Adams were muzzle loaders, the balls being loaded into the front of the cylinder and fired by a percussion cap.

4. Small calibre ball, commonly used in pocket pistols, but also of similar size to buck shot still produced for modern shotguns.

5. Mid-19th century bullet. Still muzzle-loaded, but designed for a rifled barrel. Some large calibres such as .577 were produced.

6. 20th century .45 calibre bullet.

7. 20th century .303 steel-jacketed round.

8. Flanged base of a British rifle cartridge.

9. Recessed base of a European or American cartridge. 20mm cannon shells are frequent finds near old airfields or crash sites.

10. 19th century 12 bore pinfire cartridge. These persisted into the early 20th century.

11. 20th century 12 bore cartridge. Many local gunsmiths loaded their own cases, and their headstamps can provide an added collecting interest.

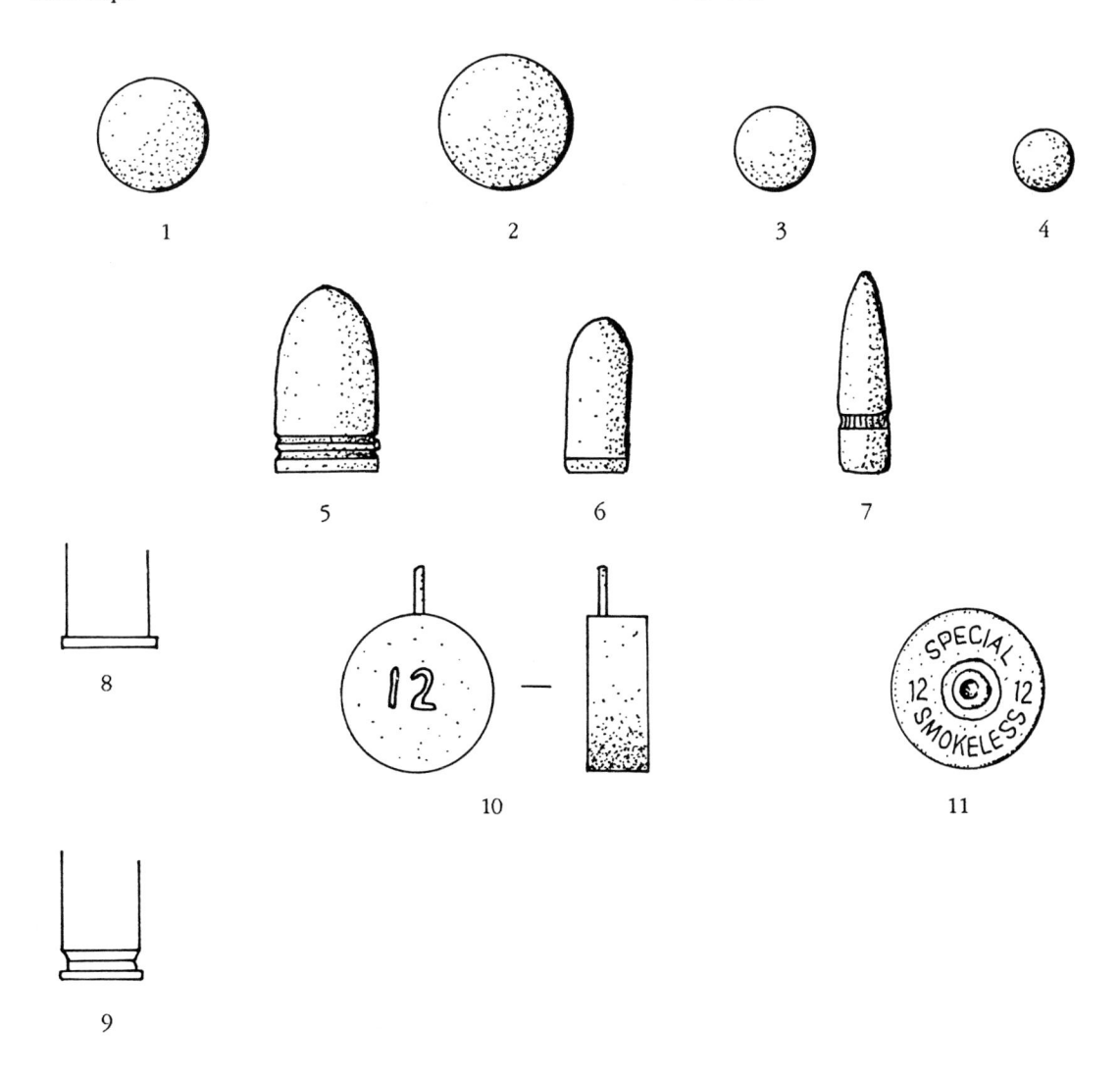

BELLS

As well as the large examples used in churches from the Middle Ages, small bells have been used as personal and harness adornment since at least Roman times.

1. Roman period bell, but difficult to date if no associated material. May have been from harness or a domestic pet, or perhaps worn by dancers.

2. Medieval rumbler bell (also commonly referred to as 'crotal' bells). Rumbler bells were attached uppermost on harness, sometimes in rows set in leather cups, and produced a 'rumbling' noise as opposed to the ringing sound of a suspended bell. Medieval examples are not common, and are generally made from metal sheet with a folded over attachment loop.

3. Cast rumbler bell with sound holes in the side and the loop an integral part of the casting. This slightly decorated example is circa 17th century.

4. Another with moulded decoration and a bell founders symbol, a 't' or hammer. 17th - 18th century.

5. Another variety with 'scale' decoration. Many plainer examples exist, and may have the founders name or initials on the base. Some known makers were Edward Seller of York (c 1678 - 1760) and Robert Wells of Aldbourne, Wilts. These 'RW' bells date from c1760 to 1826.

6. Harness bell of conventional shape, of heavily tinned brass. Embossed makers mark 'T'. 18th century. (Scale 2:3).

7. Although rumblers survive well in the ground, the conventional bell-shaped examples don't. Fragments like this often turn up.

8 and 9. By the 19th century, rumbler bells had given way to suspended bells, seen here on terret mounts. Made from stamped brass, the round example is quite different from the earlier cast types, with a screw fitting instead of a tying loop, and often stamped with the maker's name and a number, being the size of the bell relating to the maker's catalogue. (Scale 1:2).

Many small round bells turn up, either in silver or brass, and are difficult to date. Medieval hawking bells are known, and similar types may have been used by morris dancers. They were also used for babies rattles from the 18th century.

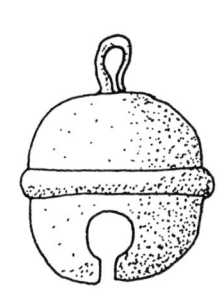

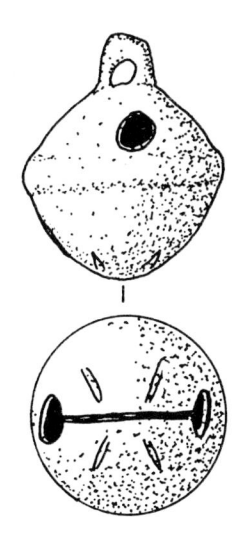

Bells

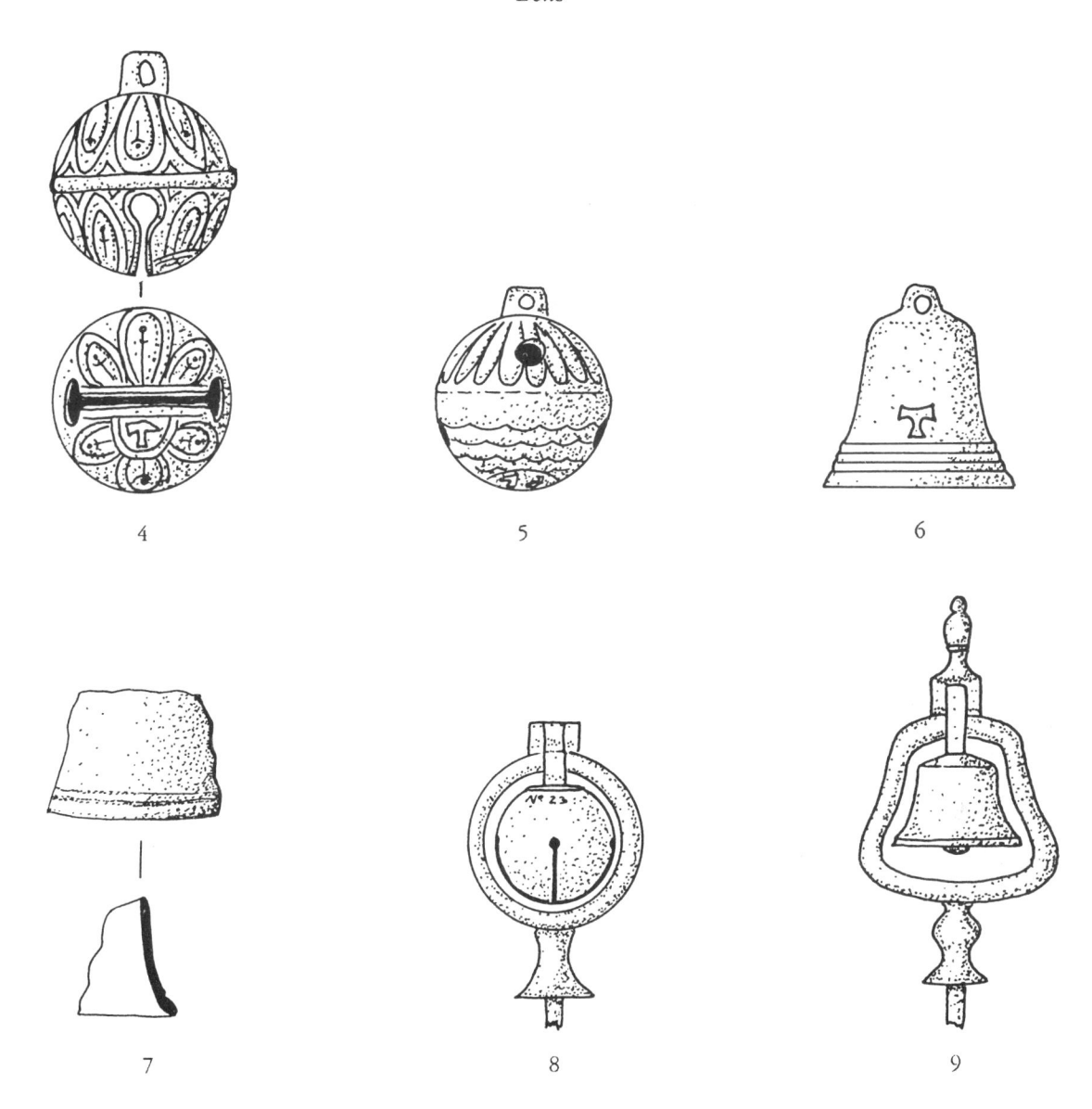

BRONZE AGE FINDS

These are treated as a distinct class of artefact, as apart from gold jewellery, bronze, or more strictly speaking copper-alloy, was the only metal used in this period. Thus any axehead or spearhead or indeed any tool made from copper-alloy will in all probability date from this time, after which period iron was used for such implements. As well as the distinctive artefacts illustrated here, a large range of other articles such as harness rings and decorative fittings have been found in hoards of metal dating from this period, but in many cases they can only be attributed by their association with more obvious items. The basic forms shown here are subject to many varieties, and occuring as chance finds many will be fragmentary. (Numbers 1 to 10 not to scale).

1. Early Bronze Age flat axe.

2. Flanged axe.

3. Palstave. A development of the flanged axe but with a hafting stop across. This example has a distinctive 'shield' pattern, but many do not.

4. Looped palstave with loop for tying to haft.

5. Socketed axe. The haft fits into the hollow body. Most but not all have tying loops.

6. A ribbed dagger.

7. A tanged spearhead.

8. A socketed spearhead.

5

9. Another with tying loops.

10. A typical sword of the period, but many variations of style exist.

11. A broken flat axe.

12. The blade section of a socketed axehead.

13. Another plough-damaged socketed axehead.

14. Broken butt-end of a palstave.

15. A sword blade fragment.

16. Typical socketed axehead. Many varieties occur, some with ribbed decoration.(Scale 1:2).

17. A socketed gouge. Chisels of similar appearance may be found, the only difference being the absence of the cut-out. (Scale 1:2)

18. Fragmentary gouge. (Scale 1:2).

19. A tanged chisel. Again many variations of form.

20. A lugged chisel with one lug. (Scale 2:3).

21. A fragment of a looped and socketed spearhead. (Scale 1:2).

22. The tip of a spearhead. (Scale 1:2).

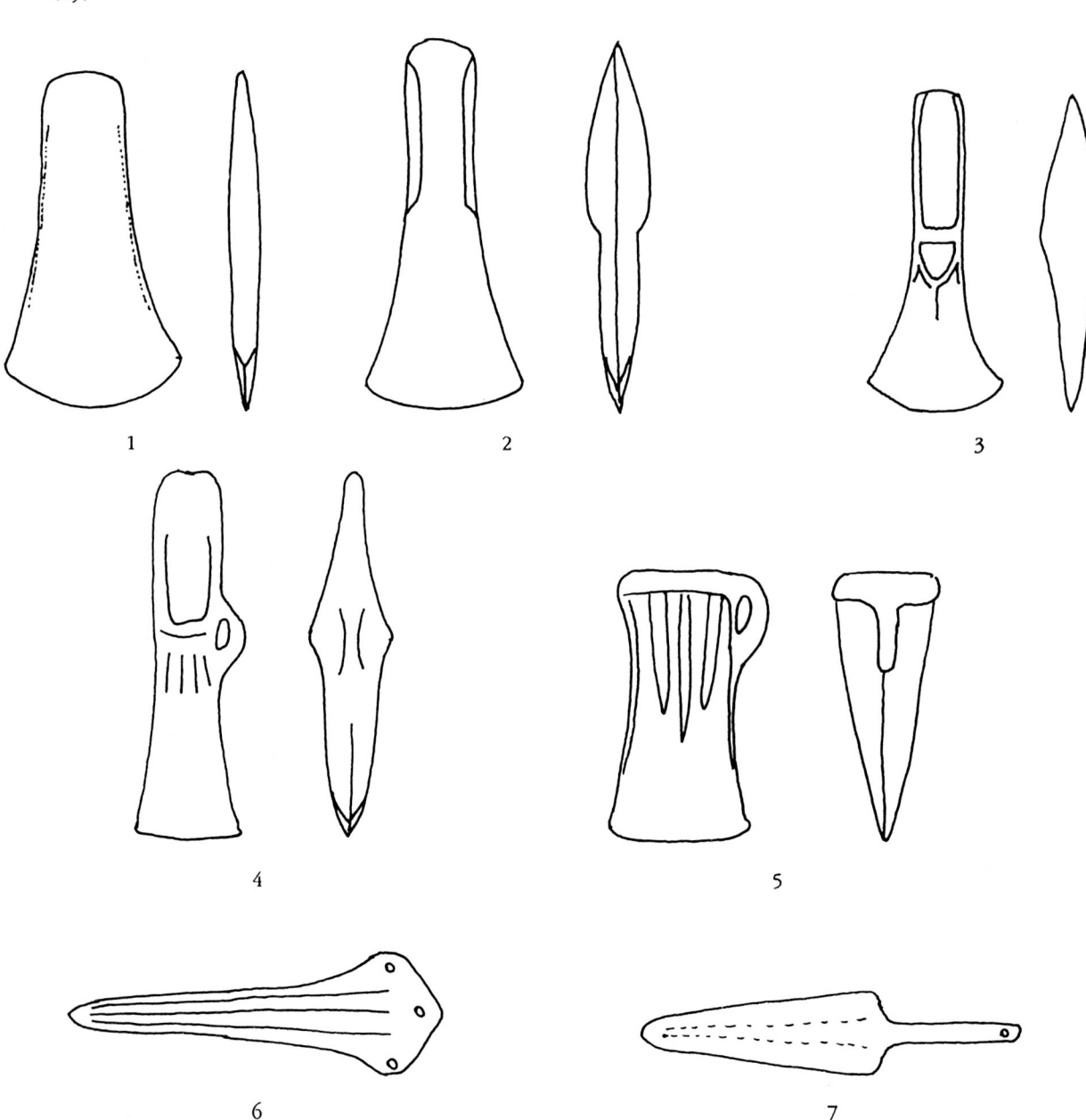

Bronze Age Finds

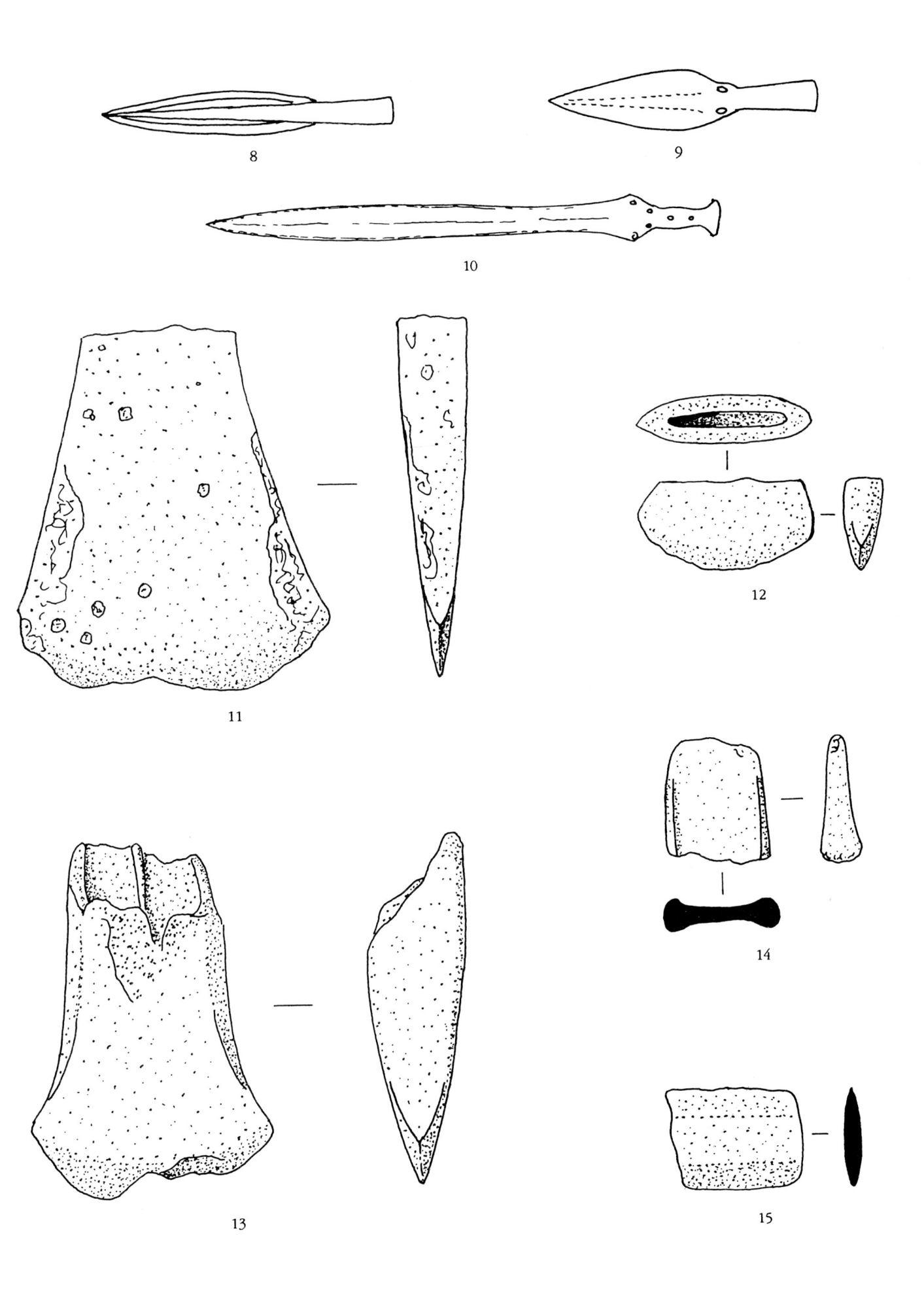

7

Bronze Age Finds

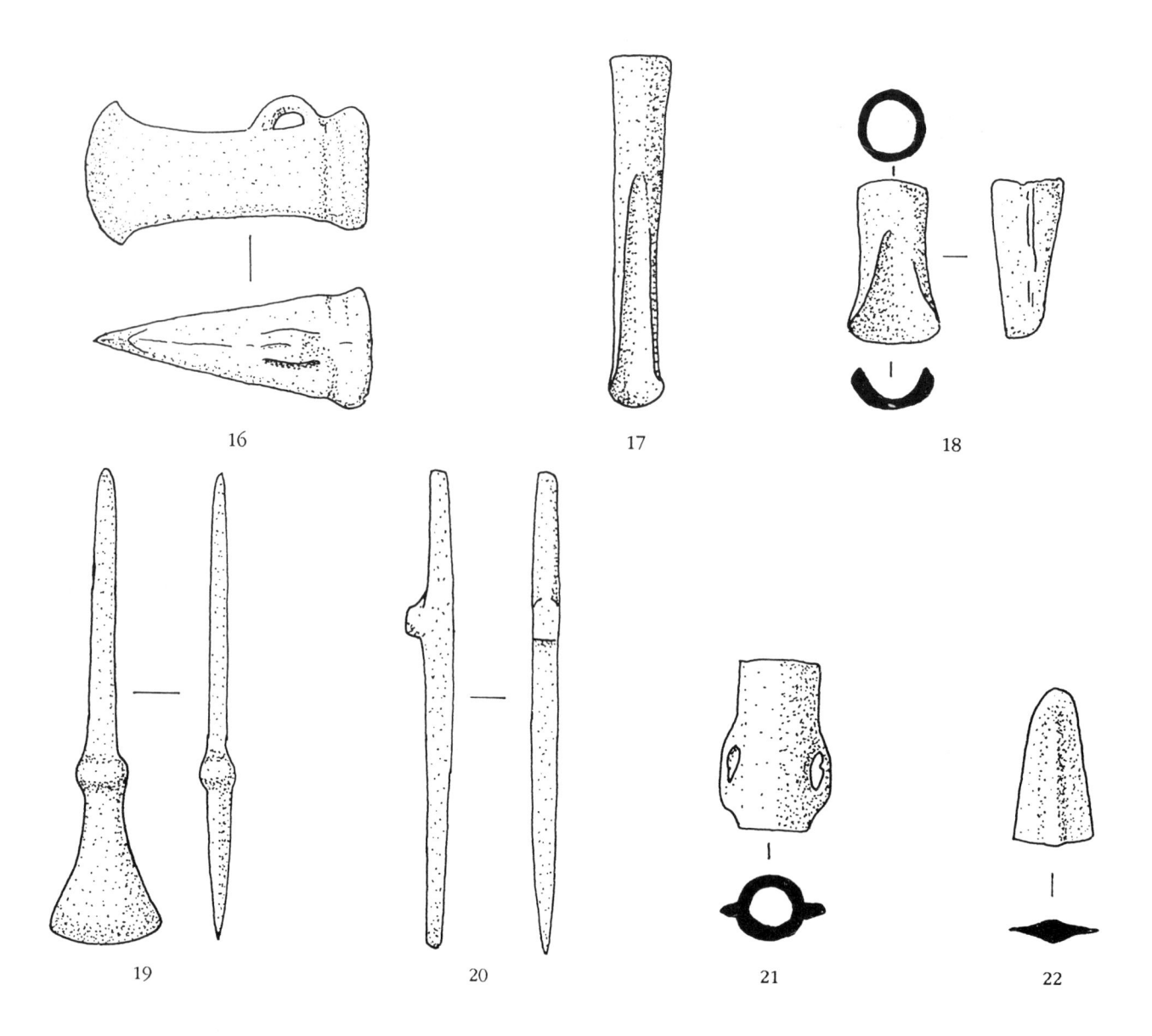

16   17   18

19   20   21   22

BUCKLES

A comprehensive corpus of buckles would fill several volumes. Various publications have included sections on them described along with other artefacts, but only a few selective studies of buckles have been published to date. This survey can only illustrate a few of the many varieties, but will hopefully serve as a guide to allow most types to be classified to at least a basic level. Recent examples are not included, as they can usually be recognised as being of machine-made manufacture, although some agricultural harness types have been illustrated. All are copper-alloy unless otherwise stated.

The earliest buckles found in Britain date to the Roman period. They have been found in Iron Age burials, but unlike purely native fittings, they cannot be distinguished from Roman types, and were either copied or imported. Roman period buckles are by no means common site finds, and are generally thought to be associated with military or official civilian regalia, rather than as general items of dress.

1. A pelta shaped buckle. This would date from the 1st century AD.

2. A one-piece pelta strap end buckle of the 2nd century.

3. Cuirass buckle of the 1st century AD. The 'D' shaped buckle was secured by a separate pin, distinguishing them from medieval types of similar appearance.

4 and 5. Zoomorphic types became popular in the 4th century, and are conjecturally associated with Saxon mercenary troops. These are one-piece strap ends.

6. Zoomorphic two-piece buckle of the late 4th - early 5th century with belt plate. (Scale 2:3).

7. Another variety of the same period. Examples are known with the loop and belt plate cast as one with a hole in the belt plate for the tongue.

8 and 9. Late 4th - early 5th century types, the zoomorphic elements now highly stylised, and now at the cross-bar position.

10. A 6th century Saxon buckle. The tongue is cast as one with the belt plate, which is riveted to a separate frame. Highly elaborate examples are known with heavy gilding and filigree decoration. (Scale 2:3).

11. A 6th or 7th century type with distinctive 'shield' shaped tongue. (Scale 2:3).

12. 6th or 7th century buckle and belt plate of Byzantine style, possibly a Merovingian import. (Scale 2:3).

13 and 14. Anglo-Scandinavian types of the 8th and 9th centuries. One piece and with zoomorphic terminals at the bar ends. (Scale 2:3).

15. A one-piece zoomorphic buckle which was riveted to the strap. Circa 9th - 10th century. (Scale 2:3).

16. 13th - 14th century with distinctive projections.

17 and 18. 13th - 14th century types with characteristic projections.

19 and 20. Of similar date, but with incised decoration.

21. Large ring-buckle of 13th - 14th century date. Annular brooches may be distinguished by having a recess for the pin, which is generally sharp enough to penetrate fabric.

22. One piece type of circa 12th -14th century.

23 and 24. 14th -15th century varieties with separate tongue rests.

25. 14th -15th century type showing frame for buckle plate.

26. Similar style and date but with plate in situ.

27. Typical 'pointed D' buckle of 14th -15th century.

28. Another with plate attached.

29. Same date range but square buckle frame.

30. 14th -15th century Composite buckle. This example was crimped to an iron strap on the underside, others had locking arms attached to the pivot.

31. 14th -15th century type with rotating tongue rest.

32. This is not a buckle in the true sense, but is in fact a locking clasp which secured a strap end.

33. 14th -15th century type with separate belt loop.

34. Large 15th century variety with bold patterning. (Scale 2:3).

35. Large 'spectacle buckle' of 15th - 16th century date. The basic 'spectacle' form dates from perhaps the 14th century through to the 17th, and is very difficult to date with any accuracy.

36 and 37. 'Spectacles' of 15th -16th century date.

38 and 39. Plain crude examples. A similar one came from the wreck of HMS Association lost in 1707.

40 - 45. All circa 16th - 17th century.

46. 16th century type with lunette projection.

47 - 49. 16th -17th century varieties.

50. Another type of similar date.

51. Square frame type of 16th - 17th century.

52 and 53. White metal types of mid-17th century.

54. Spur buckle of mid 17th century. (Scale 2:3).

55. Another probable spur buckle of similar date.

56 and 57. More ornate round 17th century types.

58. One-piece type of the later 17th century.

59. Frame of an ornate two-piece buckle in white metal. Late 17th century.

60. 18th century two-piece white metal buckle with separate tongue and strap hook.

61 and 62. Two more varieties of 18th century two-piece types.

Buckles

63 - 66. Different styles of tongue and strap hooks. These often occur as separate field finds, and sometimes have a makers stamp.

67. Plain 18th century type; one of the commonest forms occuring in all sizes.

68 and 69. Ornate late 18th century stamped brass types.

70. Steel cut variety of late 18th - early 19th century.

71. Plain rectangular type, 18th - 19th century.

72 to 76. The large ornate buckles of the 18th century rarely survive intact in ploughed land, but a collection of fragments still provides a catalogue of the wide range of designs.

77 to 85. Large harness strap buckles of mid 19th - early 20th century date. (Not to scale).

86. Sections of heavy harness strap types.

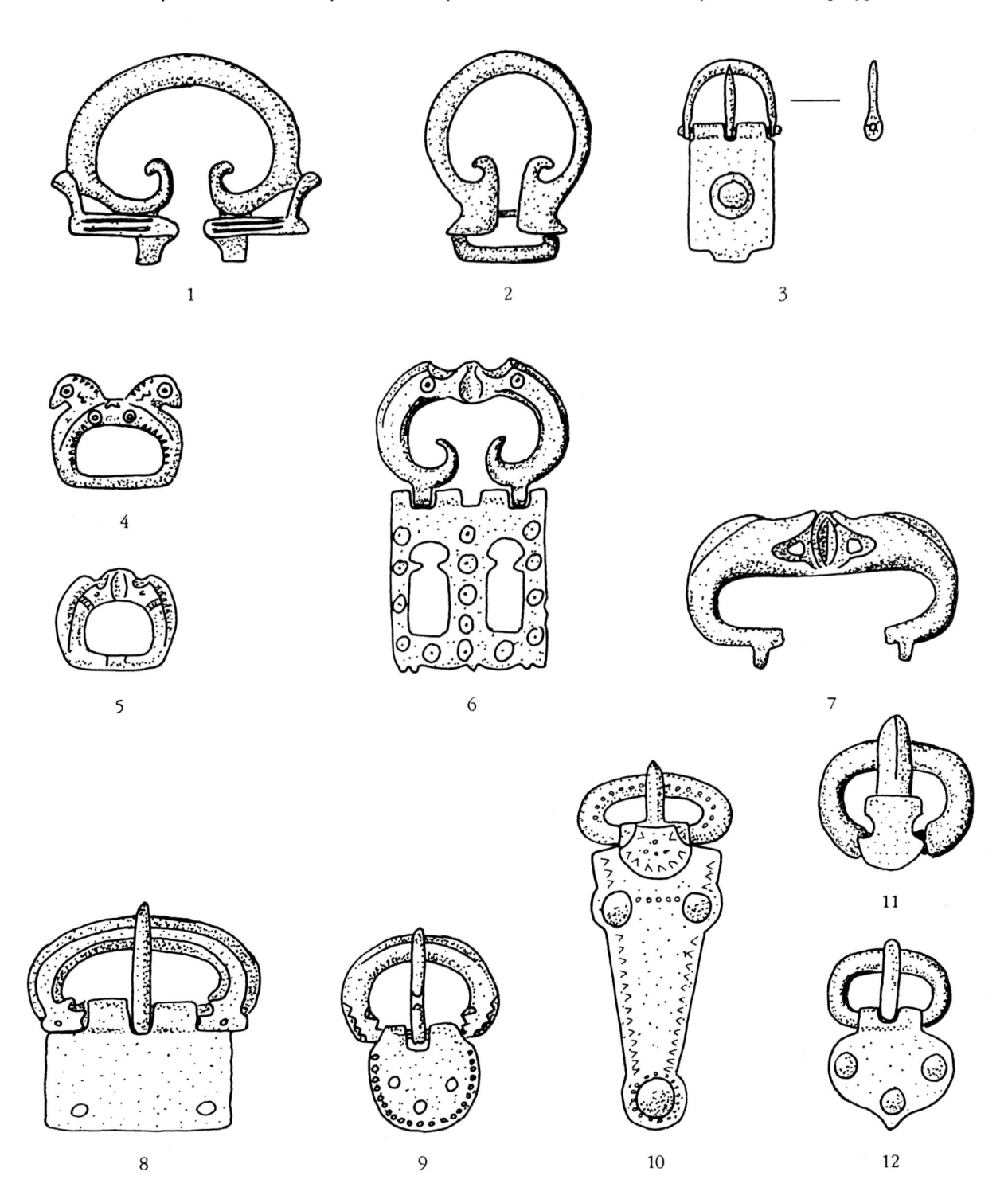

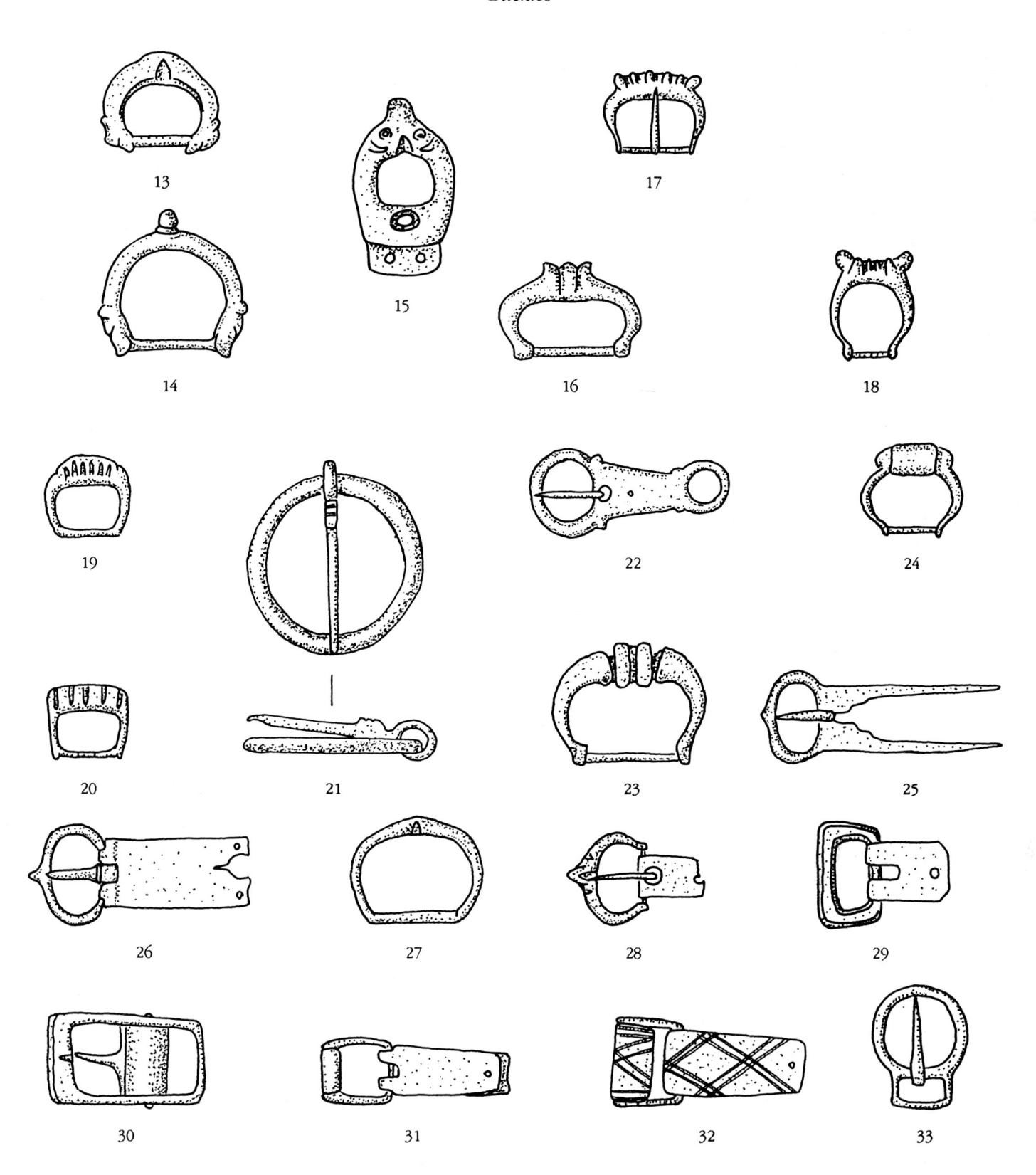

Buckles

13
14
15
16
17
18
19
20
21
22
23
24
25
26
27
28
29
30
31
32
33

11

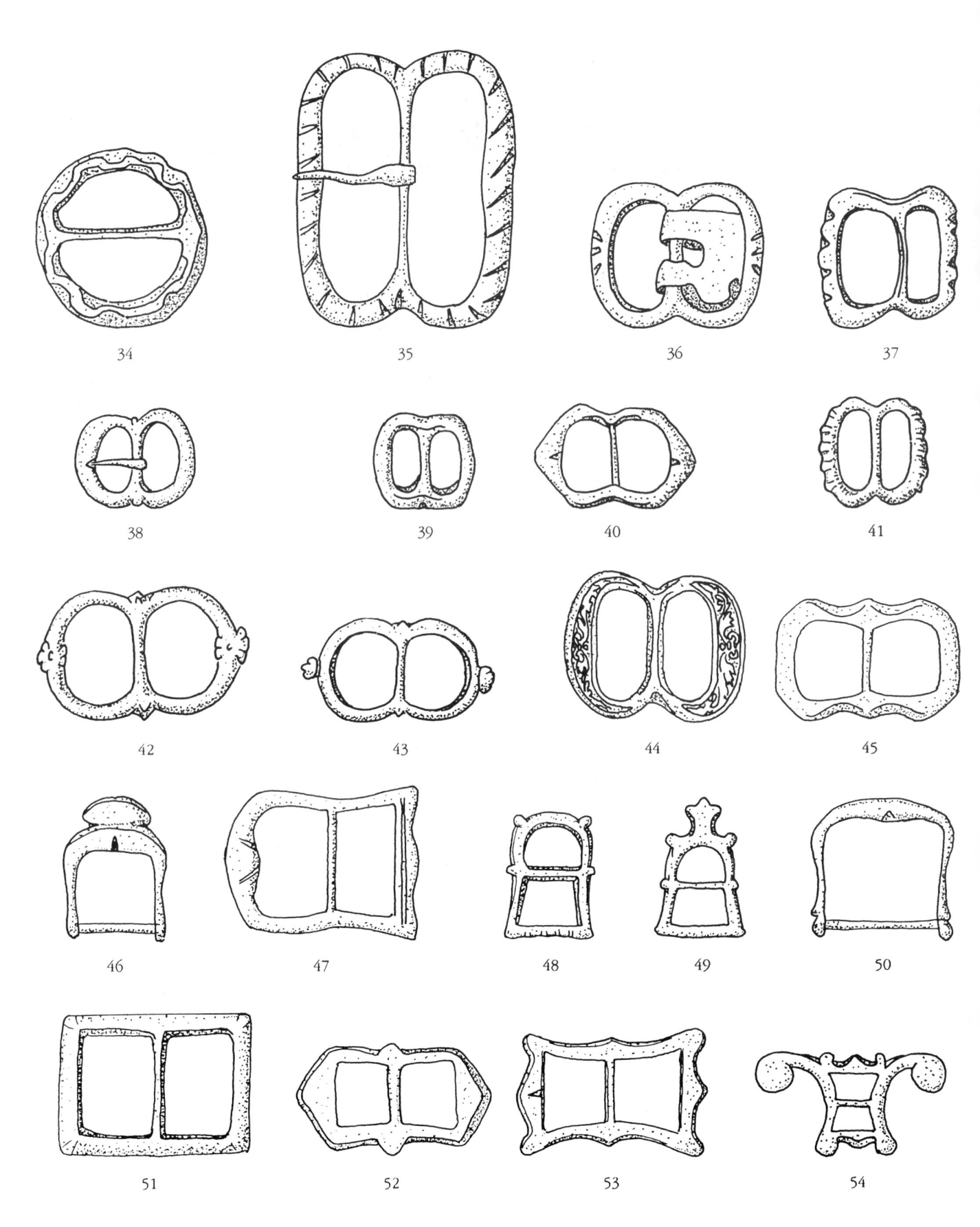

Buckles

34

35

36

37

38

39

40

41

42

43

44

45

46

47

48

49

50

51

52

53

54

Buckles

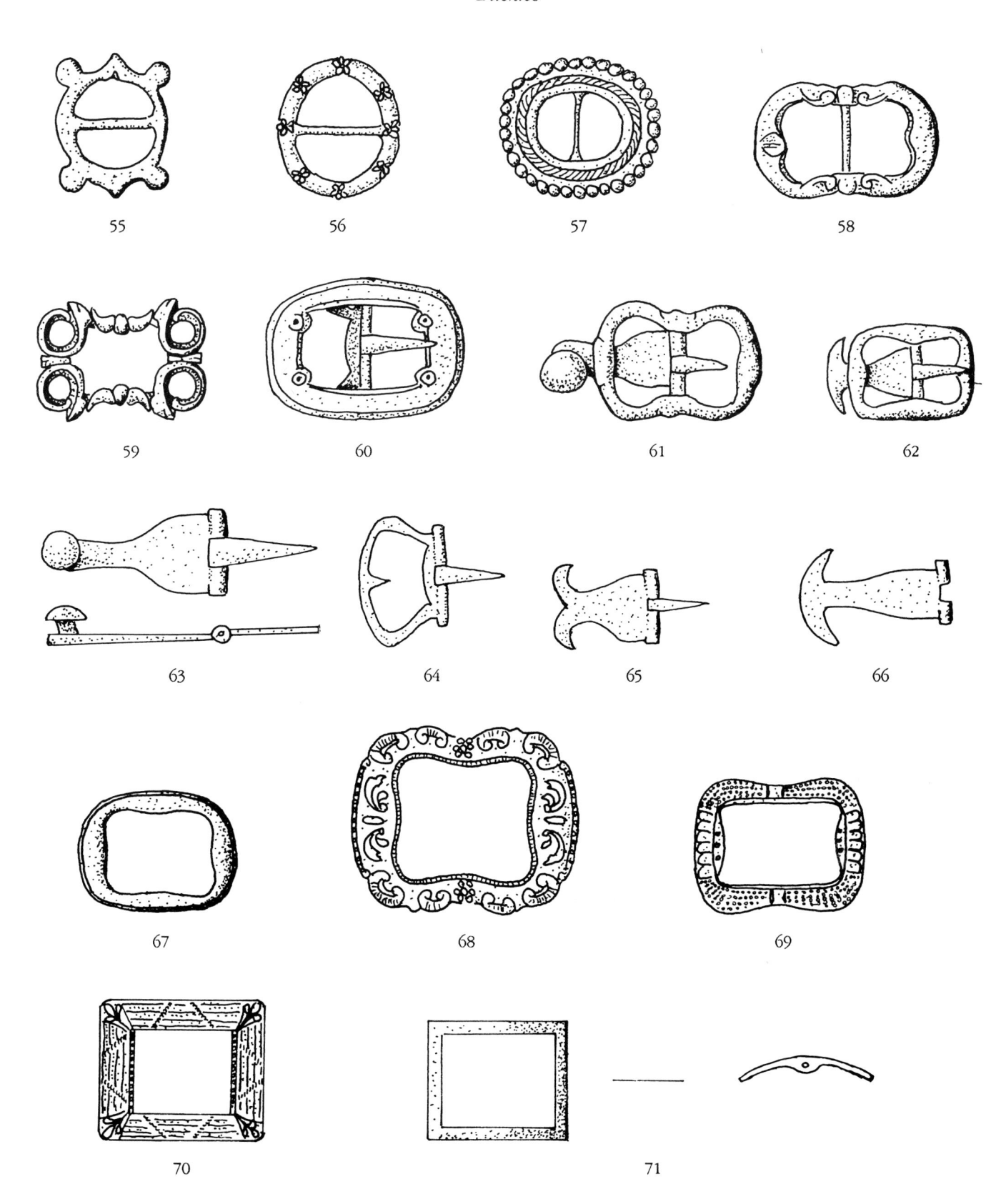

55

56

57

58

59

60

61

62

63

64

65

66

67

68

69

70

71

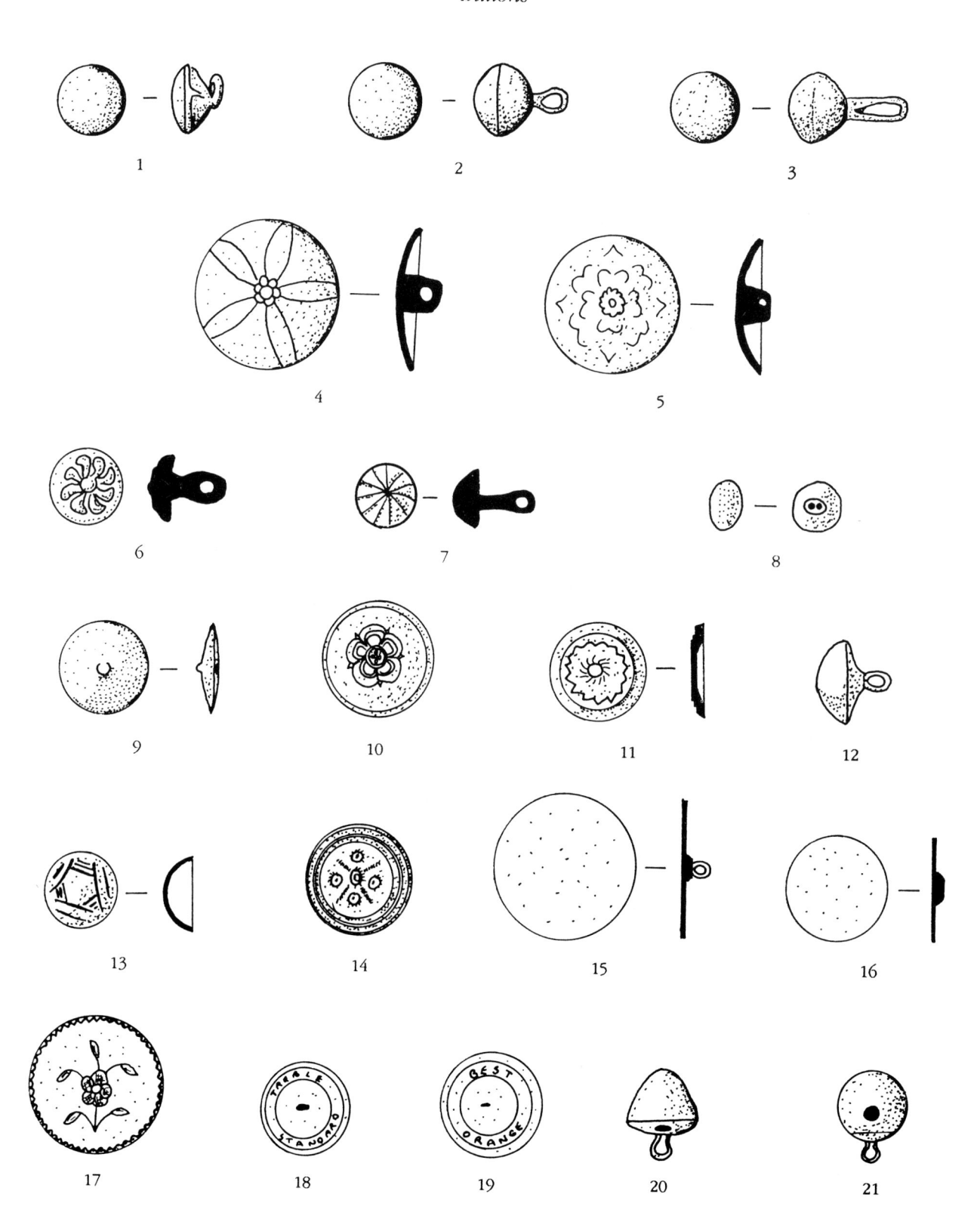

Buttons

16

Buttons

22

23

24

Buttons

25

26

27

Buttons

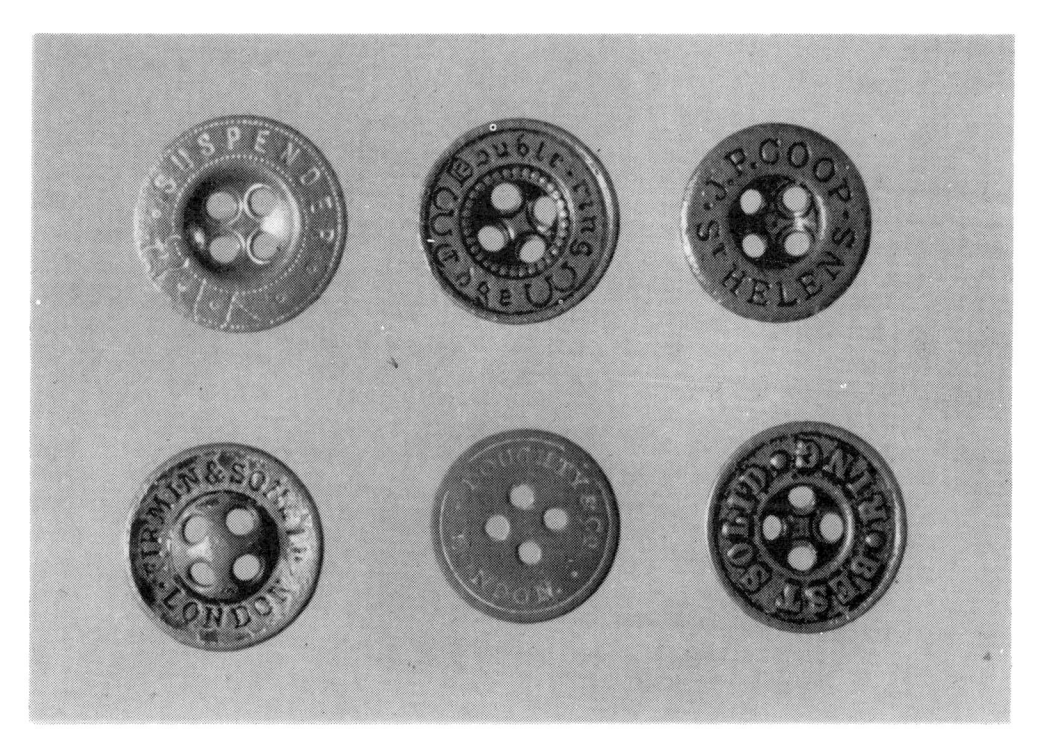

28

29

CLASPS AND FASTENERS

A great number of hooks and catches exist from all periods, but the following are all distinctive types.

1. A toggle of Late Iron-Age or Early Roman date. More elaborate enamelled examples are known, but most follow this basic form.

2. 'Wrist clasp' of the Early to Middle Saxon period. Very elaborate 'chip-carved' examples also exist.

3. Another similar 'wrist-clasp', this example has a loop into which a corresponding hooked clasp (as previous) would locate.

4. A plain example of the same period.

5. An Early - Middle Saxon fastener made from coiled bronze wire.

6 to 8. Clothing hooks of the Late Saxon to early medieval periods. No. 8 may be based on the design of an Arabic coin. They are attached by piercings in the plate.

9 to 12. Late medieval to Tudor types. Distinguished by an attachment loop.

13. A late to post-medieval book clasp of common form. This was attached to a strap secured to the book by a fitting (14) on one cover, and hooked around another fitting (15) on the other.

16 and 17. Two further varieties of book clasp. Various styles of incised decoration also occur.

18 and 19. 17th - 18th century small clasps, probably from books but also possibly shoes.

20. Shoe or clog clasp. 18th century. This has a tongue for securing to the strap distinguishing the type from book clasps.

21. Larger plain example 18th century.

22. Stamped brass shoe clasp of 18th -19th century. This is a catch corresponding to the hooks on the previous two.

23. Large example secured by four rivets on the inside. Circa 1800. This type was used on military neck-stocks of the Napoleonic period, and similar two-piece catches were still in use on cycling shoes of the late 19th to early 20th centuries, although these were made of lacquered steel.

24. Looking like a small keyhole escutcheon, this is a stay busk of 19th -20th century date. They were used to secure the steel stays on corsets, and normally retain a small blob of rust behind the rivets.

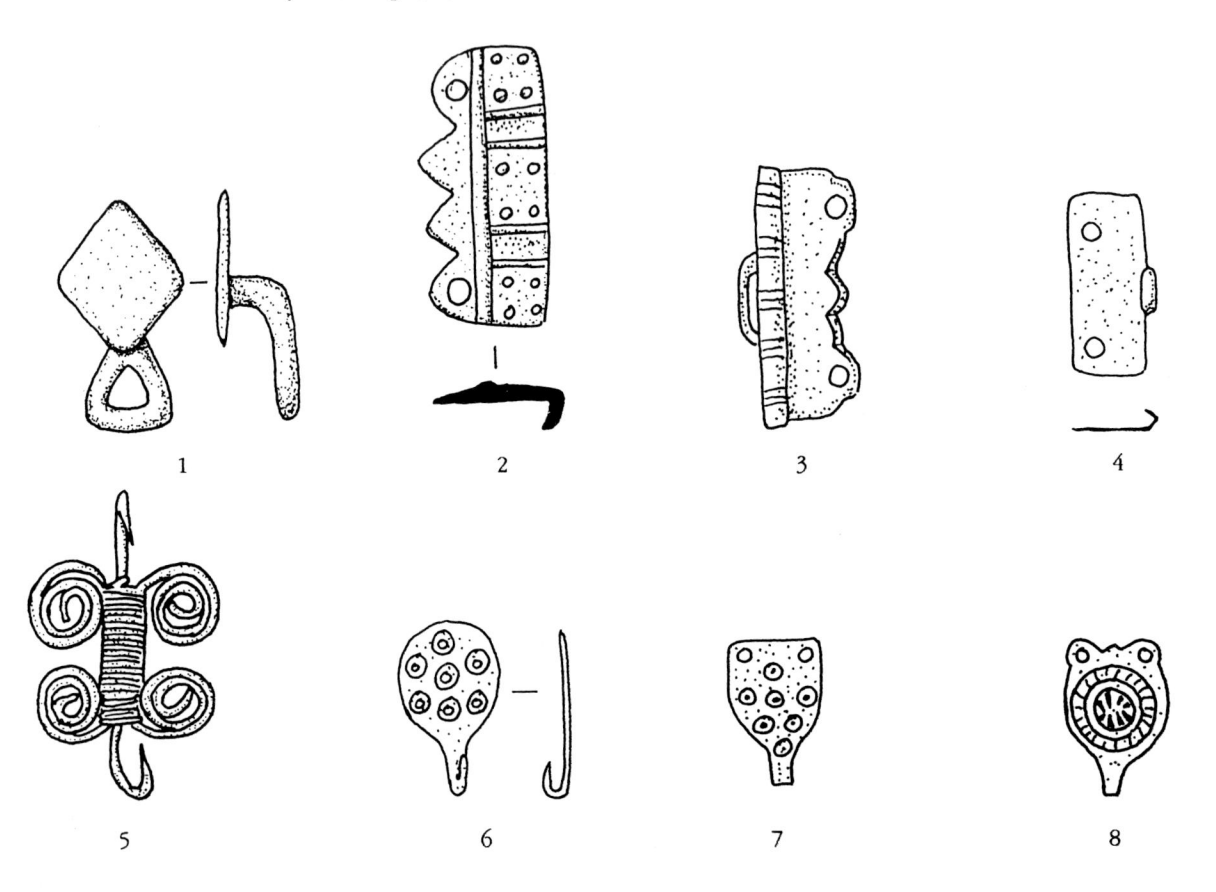

Clasps and Fasteners

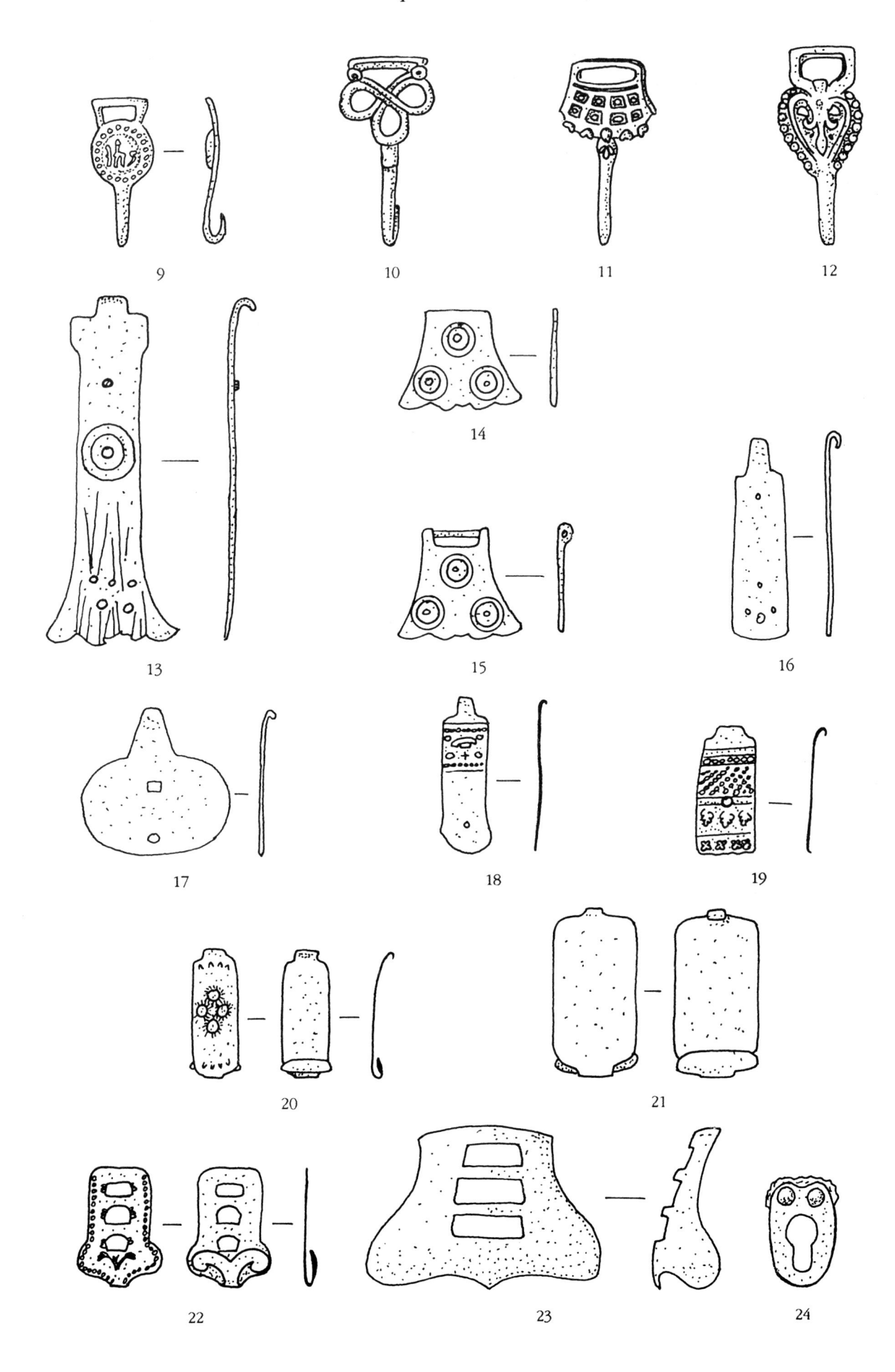

9 10 11 12

13 14 15 16

17 18 19

20 21

22 23 24

HORSESHOES

The function of the horseshoe is to protect the hoof from wear and damage when it comes into contact with hard surfaces, and so it is not surprising that they are first encountered in the Roman Period, when a vast network of metalled roads were constructed. The odd thing however, is that despite this, horseshoes of the conventional type cannot be attributed to the Roman period with any certainty, and even on the sites of presumed cavalry forts no definitely stratified examples seem to have been recovered. The only horseshoes that are certainly Roman in date are the so-called 'hippo sandals' which were apparently tied on to the hoof, and these occur on rural sites well away from the surfaced military roads as well as more likely locations. None of the illustrations are to scale.

1. This is a so-called 'hippo-sandal' and is quite distinctive, although rarely surviving intact on ploughed land.

2. All that is usually identifiable of a plough-damaged hippo sandal is the wing and hook rear section.

3. This wavy-edged type has been referred to as 'Celtic' on account of examples recovered in late Iron Age contexts. This may or may not be the case, and it would depend on the reliability of the context in being sealed from later intrusion, but the type can be attributed with a fair degree of certainty to the 11th and 12th centuries.

4. This is a similar light-weight shoe but without the wavy edge. It still has recessed nail holes and calkins, and probably dates from the 12th to 14th centuries.

5. This type of heavy horseshoe is known as a 'Guildhall' shoe. These range roughly from the 13th to 15th centuries, and tend to be curved in section with a thick fore-end and the inner arch terminating in a point. They may occur with no calkins, or with one or two.

6. Another Guildhall shoe with one calkin. The number of nail holes can vary from six to 10 depending on the size of the shoe, but larger numbers are assumed to be later in date coinciding with the development of heavier horses for both civil and military use.

7. This is a light shoe of simple crescent form known as a 'Dove' shoe, and they range from perhaps the 13th to the 16th centuries. They may occur with six or seven nail holes, and may have calkins.

8. This type is known as a 'keyhole' horseshoe on account of its shape, this example also being fullered, which is a groove running around part and sometimes all of the circumference. These date from around the 16th to 17th centuries.

9. A heavy shoe with 'keyhole' characteristics, probably 16th or 17th century in date.

10. Following on from the 'keyhole', this type is known as a 'tongue' shoe on account of the shape of the centre opening. These are generally dated to the 16th and 17th centuries, but some may also be contemporary with the 'Guildhall' shoes, as the form is generally the same except for the shape of the inner opening, which one suspects may sometimes be the result of individual blacksmithing rather than a definite chronological characteristic.

11. This is an 18th to 19th century type manufactured from a regular bar of metal, with fullering and 8 nail holes. By the 19th century 7 holes were general although not exclusive, and the shoes were regular in form.

12. A typical 'cart horse' shoe with toe clips. Many varieties occur to regular designs and cover the 19th to early 20th centuries.

13. Another 19th - 20th century type with fullering and calkins. Both these latter types continued in use up until the demise of horse traffic and agricultural use.

14. The most commonly found modern shoe is pre-formed with toe-clips and fullering, and is adjusted for fit by the farrier as required.

15. Ox shoes may be confused with broken horseshoes unless in good condition, and generally cannot be dated with any certainty. The use of oxen for ploughing and draught use dates from medieval times to the 18th century. Small regular 'horseshoes' may be from small ponies, but also the heel plates of heavy boots!

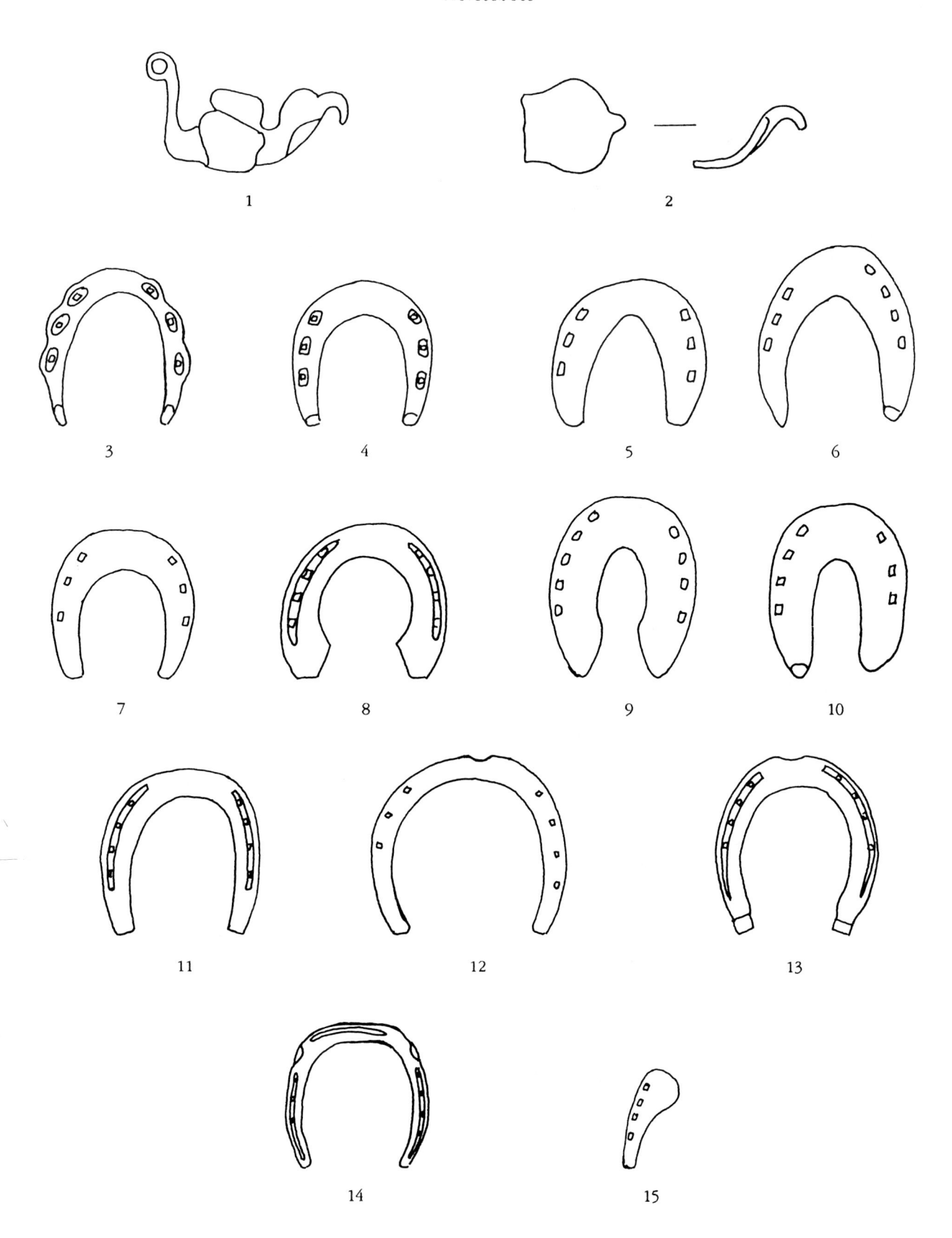

Horseshoes

JEWELLERY

Jewellery of one form or another has been popular from the Early Stone Age, with shells being worn as pendants or necklaces, and with the development of metalworking it became possible to manufacture a wide variety of objects. Raw gold was probably worked into ornaments at quite an early time, but in Britain its use seems to run concurrent with the development of bronze working technology. This section concentrates on general types of find, and ignores the more splendid objects which should they occur will be sufficiently impressive for the finder to realise he has something special. As with other sections in this volume, I have concentrated on older material for as the time span lessens, the range of variety and style in jewellery becomes vast, and even that which is included here only touches on a few examples.

1. Side looped pin of the Middle Bronze Age, used presumably as a clothing fastener.(Scale 1:2).

2. Quoit headed pin of the same period.(Scale 1:2).

3. Late Bronze Age violin-bow brooch, circa 10th century BC.

4. Early Iron Age Brooch circa 4th -3rd century BC. Note exposed spring and bent back foot.

5. Another example lacking both spring and foot; typical of a ploughsoil find.

6. Late Iron Age (La Tène III) brooch of late 1st century BC to early 1st century AD. The spring is still exposed.

7. One piece 'Colchester' brooch of early 1st Century AD. This example is in typical 'dug up' condition, but the complete brooch was worked entirely from one piece of metal forming the body, spring guard, spring, pin and catchplate.

8. Elaborate bracelet of the Roman period.(Scale 2:3).

9. Open section Roman period bracelet with snake design.(Scale 2:3).

10 to 13. Fragments of Roman period bracelets showing typical patterning.

14 and 15. Two bracelet fragments of the Roman period showing rouletted decoration. These were often silvered or tinned.

16. Terminal of a Roman period 'snake' bracelet.

17. Roman gold earring of typical form.

18. Plain loop earring, Roman period. Silver and gold examples are fairly common.

19. Roman period earring pendant of drop form.

20 to 23. Decorative hair and clothing pins were widely used in the Roman period, these being just a few of many styles.

24. Roman period 'dolphin' brooch of typical form. 1st century AD. Many variations.

25. 'Hod Hill' brooch of 1st century AD. Many variations.

26. Hinge headed brooch of 1st -2nd century derived from 'Hod Hill' types.

27. 'Headstud' brooch of 2nd century with loop and enamelled stud.

28. 'Knee' brooch of the 2nd century. Many varieties.

29. 'Crossbow' brooch of the 4th century.(Scale 2:3).

30. Penannular brooch of the Late Iron Age.

31. Another variety of the Roman period.

32. Disc brooch of the 2nd century AD. Enamelled centre boss on back plate with lugs. Many varieties.

33. Typical field find lacking centre boss and lugs mostly broken off.

34. Enamelled 'dragonesque' brooch of the 1st century AD.

35. Enamelled plate brooch of the 2nd century. Many varieties.

36. Another fragmented example.

37. Enamelled composite brooch with disc and plate type elements. 2nd century AD. Many varieties.

38. 'Hare and Young' plate brooch. Tinned copper-alloy with enamel inlay. 2nd century AD.

39. Another plate brooch in the form of a running hare. Many varieties, horse and rider and bird motifs being popular.

40. A glass centre boss brooch of 4th century date, this example with the paste setting now lost. These were frequently gilded on the front and tinned on the back.

Jewellery

41 and 42. Typical field finds of brooch fragments, in this case the catchplate and head of two 1st - 2nd century brooches.

43. Gold and cornelian finger ring. Gold was reserved for the upper classes of Roman society until the 3rd century AD, and thus a 1st century example such as this would be a very rare find. Classical rings were much imitated from the 18th century (see no. 78) as well as ancient gemstones being remounted in new settings from the medieval period.

44. Gold and onyx ring of the 3rd century.

45. Another gold 3rd century example with pronounced shoulders, the bezel engraved.

46. Large and heavy base silver and nicolo ring of the 2nd century. A fairly common type, the rather flattened shape of the hoop suggests that they were often worn on the first joint of a finger or thumb.

47. Tinned copper-alloy ring of Roman period. Many varieties.

48. Roman period octagonal ring, also occurring in silver or gold.

49. Saxon 'crossbow' brooch of early 5th century. Note zoomorphic terminal.

50. Saxon 'trefoil-headed' brooch of the 6th century.(Scale 2:3).

51. Saxon cruciform brooch circa 6th century.(Scale 2:3).

52. Saxon 'square-headed' brooch of similar date.(Scale 2:3).

53. 'Radiate-headed' brooch of 6th century. A European import.(Scale 2:3).

54. An 'equal-arm' brooch of similar date copying European style.

55. Saxon round brooch with 'face' design. 5th - 6th century. Often gilded or silvered.

56. 'Saucer' brooch of 5th - 6th century. Many varieties.

57. Rare disc brooch with cloisonné enamel attributed to the 10th or 11th century and if so a direct copy from the Roman style (see no. 32).

58 and 59. Field finds of Saxon period brooch fragments.

60. Silver finger ring of typical coiled form. 6th century AD.

61. Lead-alloy disc brooch of Scandanavian design. 10th century.

62. Annular brooch of 13th - 14th century date. Some are difficult to differentiate from ring-buckles, but brooches normally have retaining shoulders for the pin whereas buckles do not.

63. Ring brooch of the same period minus the pin. Only the light patterning and recess for the pin identify it as a brooch and not simply a ring for some other purpose.

64. Another of the same period with turrets for paste inserts.

65. Scarce variety of the same period. Precious metal examples of ring brooches occur.

66. Gold and a sapphire stirrup ring of the 13th century. This shape of hoop was popular during this period.

67. Gold and turquoise ring of the 15th century with claw mount. As well as 'normal' size ones like this example, many rings that occur between the 15th to 17th centuries are of small size; this does not however mean that they were worn by children, but were in fact worn on the first or second joints of the finger. Effigies and portraits demonstrate that up to twenty rings could be worn at the same time, several to a finger, and that they were even sewn onto sleeves, or worn on a cord around the neck.

68. 13th century gold and a garnet ring. The inability to cut gemstones at this period resulted in them being used 'en cabochon' or uncut, and the bezels were often adapted to the shape of the stone.

69. Bezel of a merchant's ring of the 14th -15th century. Commonly found in copper-alloy, silver and gold examples also exist; this form is usual, with an initial under a crown.

70. Silver-gilt iconographic ring of mid-15th century. The bezel is engraved with the figure of a saint.

71. 15th century silver-gilt 'fede' ring. The clasped hands symbol remained popular into the 16th century, and occurs from time to time in later periods.

72. Silver-gilt ring engraved with the stations of the cross. Religious symbolism is a common theme, with many rings of the period engraved with words or symbols.

73. Gold signet ring of the 16th century. These were popular in both gold and silver, and either bear the arms of the wearer, or his initials.

74 - 76. Inscriptions on rings and other items of jewellery sometimes occur, with the lettering often being one guide to date. Gothic or black lettering (74A) and Lombardic (74B) were popular throughout the Middle Ages, giving way to capitals by the 16th century (75). Rings were engraved on either the inside or outside, and this was particularly popular with betrothal rings which bore rhyming couplets. These poetry or 'posy' rings continued in fashion until the 18th century, after which time they went out of favour, caused in part by the requirement to stamp assay markings inside. Early examples are often inscribed on the outside of the band, later ones on the inside. By the mid-17th century script rather than capitals was normally used (76).

77. Gold and paste ring of circa 1600. By the 17th century, jewellery became more elaborate and employed enamelling as well as the use of multiple stone settings; faceting was developed in the 16th century and became more complex over the following years. 'Memento Mori' rings occur largely in the 17th and 18th centuries, sometimes with a skull motif or containing a lock of hair, and inscribed with the name and age of the deceased.

78. As mentioned earlier, ancient rings were extensively copied, and gemstones re-used. This example is gold and a garnet dating from the 18th century. The bezels often have a ridged inner ring, and occasionally were on a swivel.

79. This is a thin rolled brass ring of the 18th century, divided into decorated panels. Not to be confused with medieval 'decade' rings, which had a series of projections and were used in the same way as rosary beads.

80. A small brass ring with light scroll decoration and typical of the 19th century.

81. Not all recent rings were hallmarked; this silver signet ring is only dated by the engraving style. 19th -20th century.

82. (photograph). General low-quality jewellery, 18th century to modern.

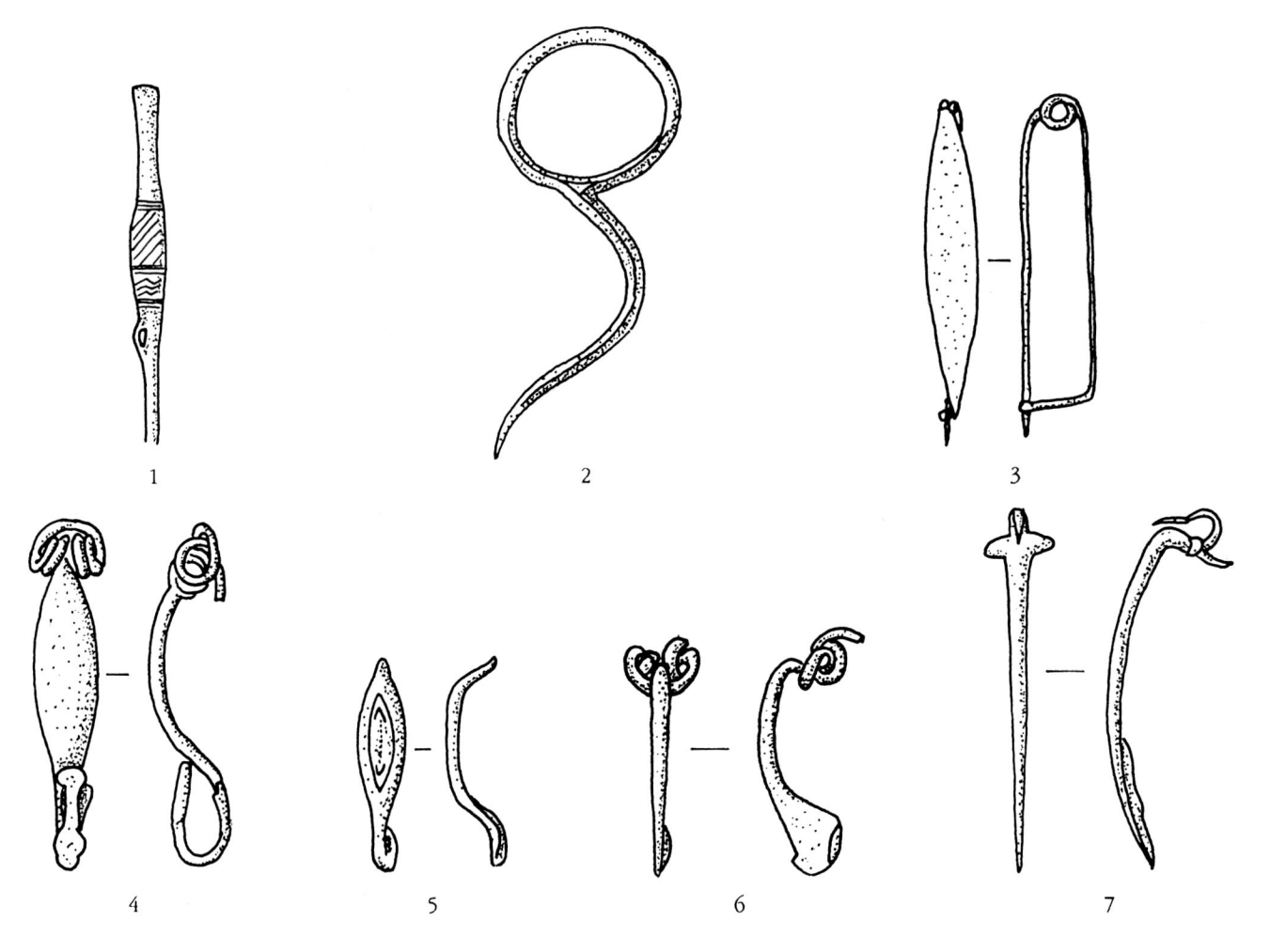

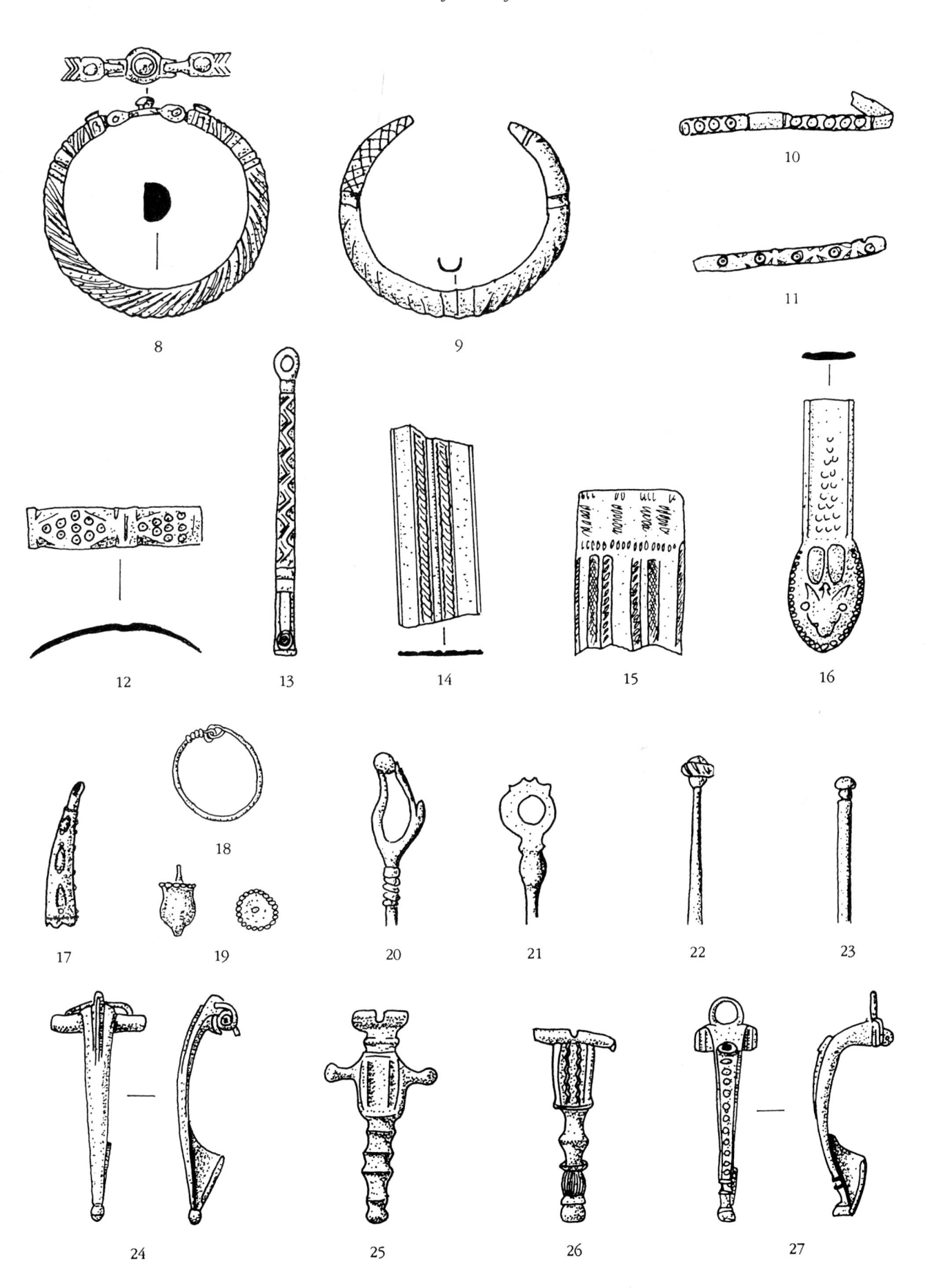

Jewellery

27

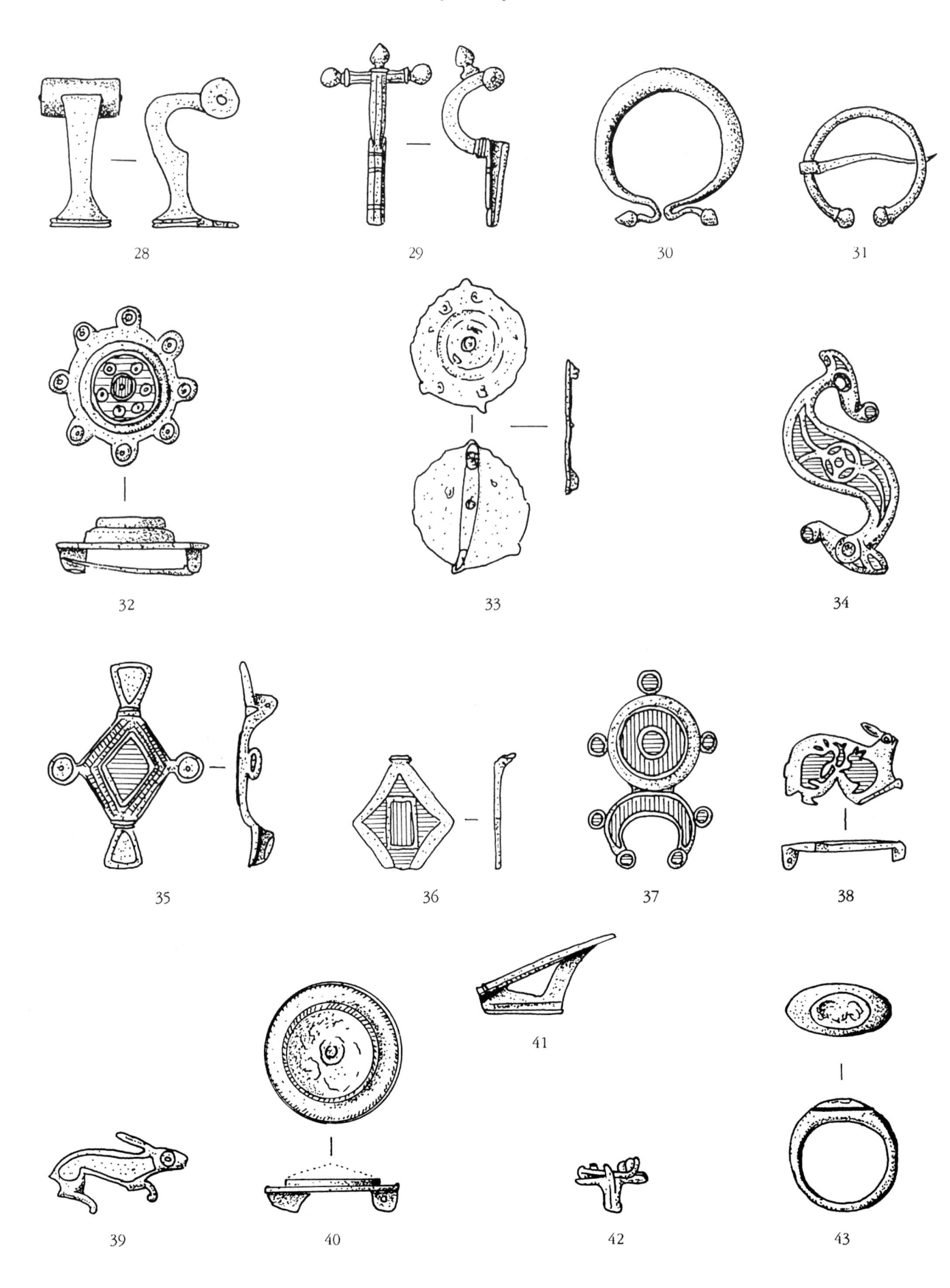

Jewellery

28 29 30 31

32 33 34

35 36 37 38

39 40 41 42 43

28

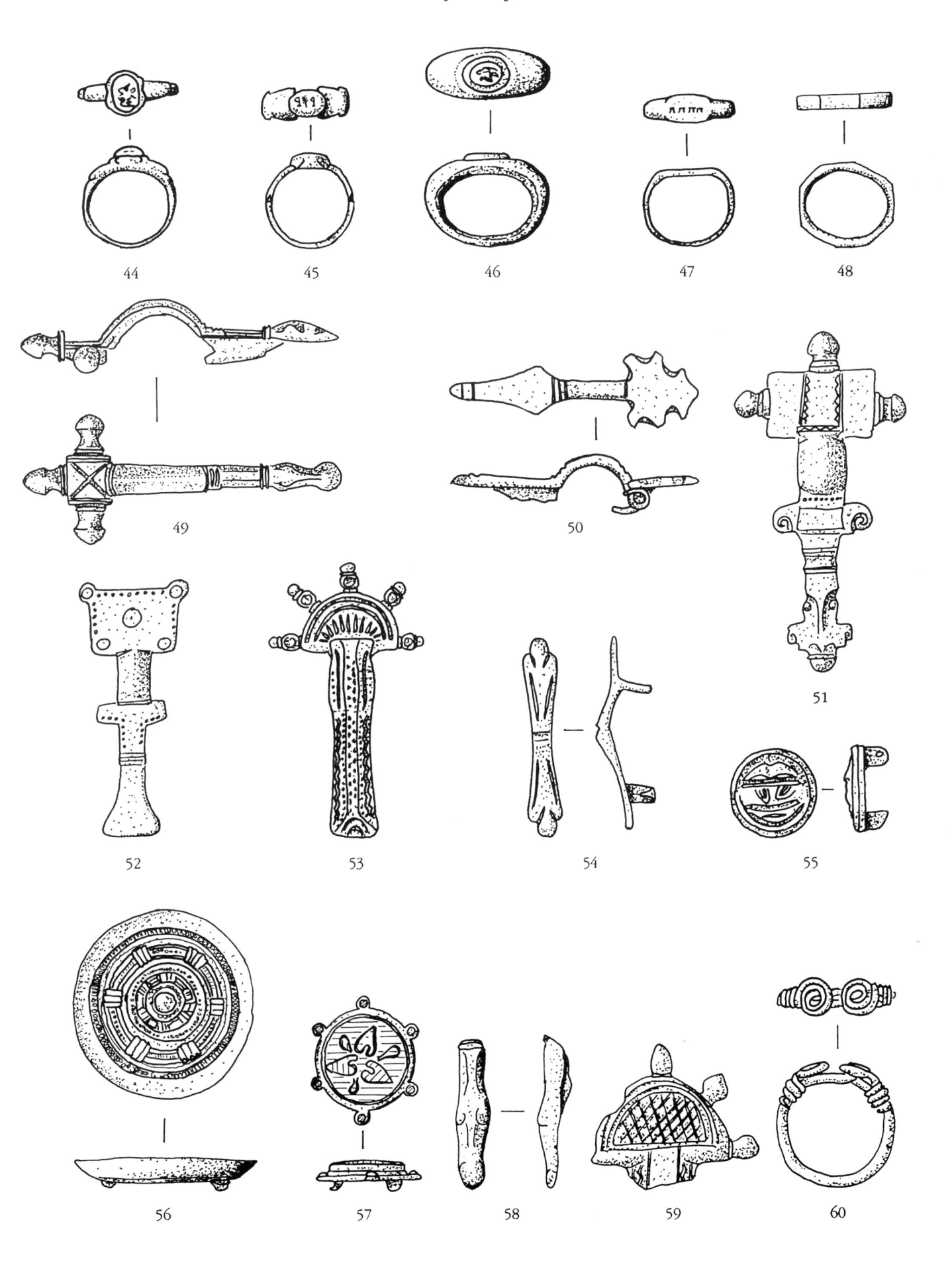

Jewellery

44 45 46 47 48

49 50 51

52 53 54 55

56 57 58 59 60

29

Jewellery

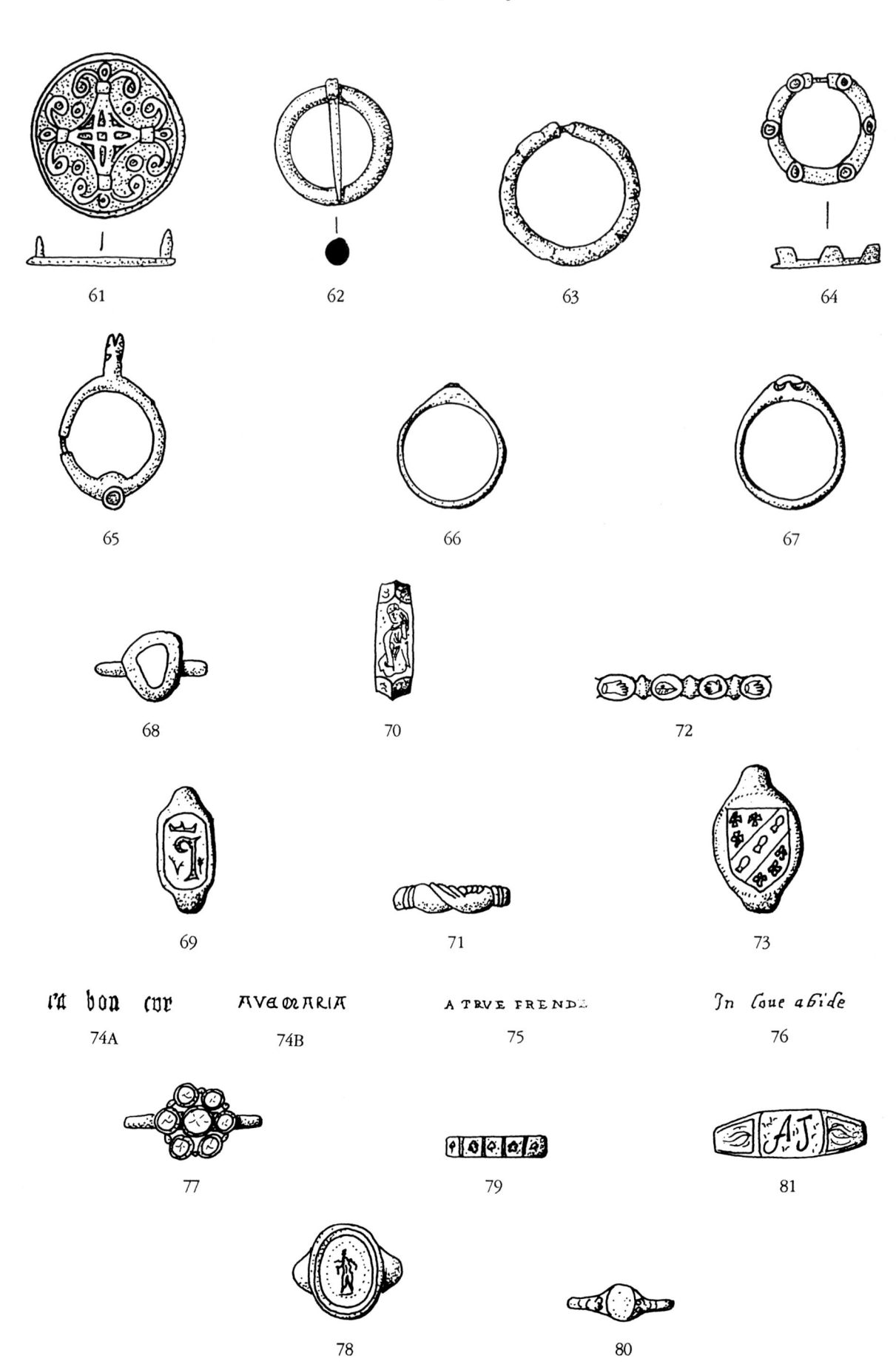

61

62

63

64

65

66

67

68

70

72

69

71

73

l'a bon cor AVE MARIA A TRVE FRENDE In loue abide
74A 74B 75 76

77

79

81

78

80

Jewellery

82

KEYS

As with so many things, keys were introduced into Britain by the Romans, although some pre-invasion imports probably exist.

1. Iron lift key. Roman period. A common find, the wards frequently broken off.(Scale 1:2).

2. Iron slide key. Roman period.The wards are projecting lugs.(Scale 2:3).

3. Copper-alloy handle from an iron key. Roman period.

4. Turn key. Most Roman examples have the handle at right-angles to the wards, and Roman keys with a vertical handle loop are difficult to separate from medieval types, but the end projection and decorated shoulders on this key are a feature of Roman types.

5. Finger-ring key. Roman period.

6. Late-Saxon to Norman period loop key.

7. Simple key of the medieval period. A wide variety of crude casket keys exist.

8. Later medieval key with lozenge head and more elaborate wards.

9. 16th - 17th century casket key. Some highly elaborate keys were produced during this period, the cutting of the wards on iron examples are works of art.

10. Iron 'ogee' door key of the 17th century.(Scale 1:2).

11. Iron door key circa 18th century. Iron door keys, particularly when rusted, are very difficult to date, and this design remains constant through to recent times. (Scale 1:2).

12. 18th -19th century night-latch key. (Scale 2:3).

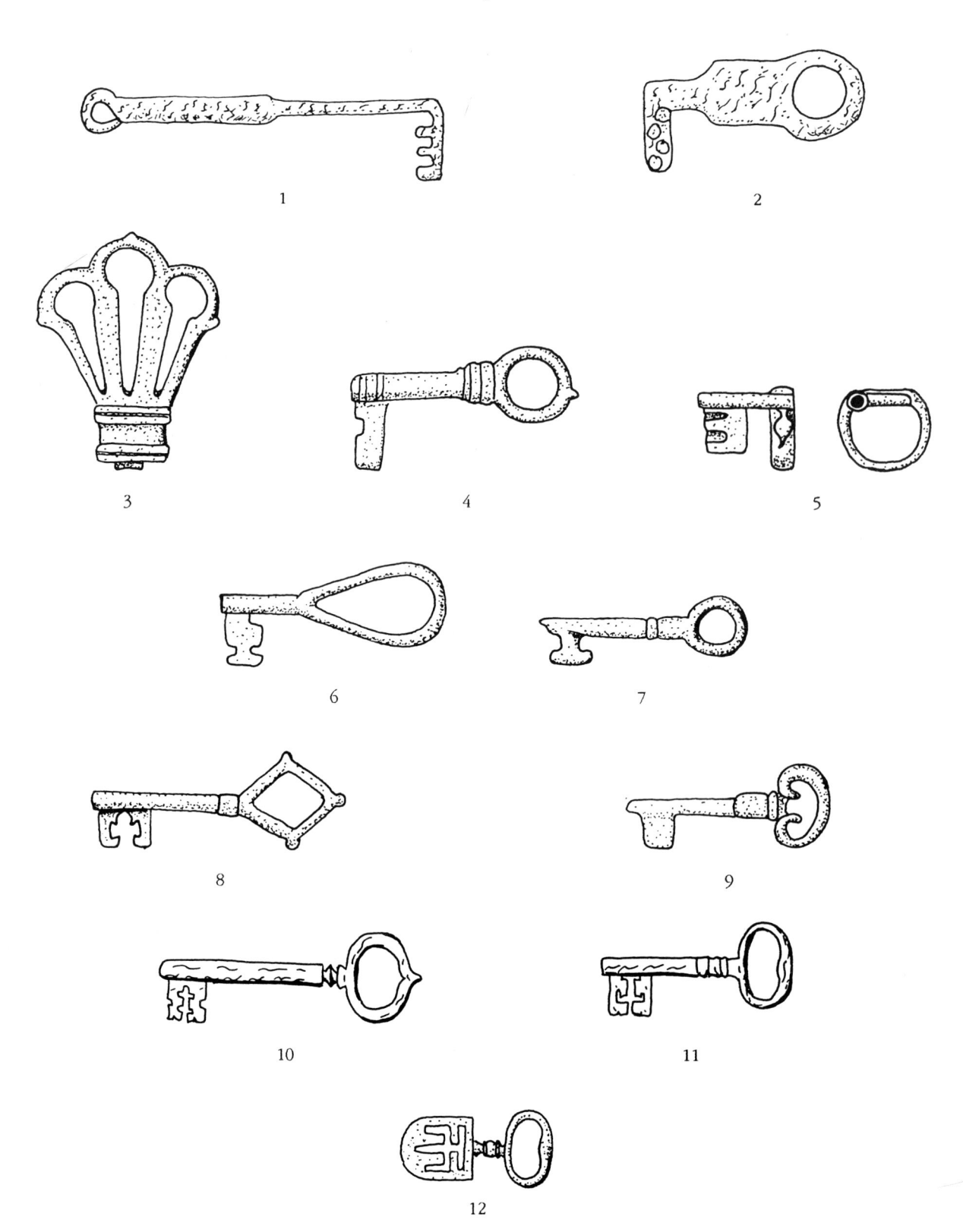

Keys

1

2

3

4

5

6

7

8

9

10

11

12

MOUNTS AND FITTINGS

This section covers a wide range of objects from all periods, including strap mounts from items of both personal and equestrian use, and also furniture fittings.

STRAP ENDS

1. Roman 'amphora' shaped strap end of the late 4th century AD.
2. Another 4th century type; note 'ring and dot' decoration.
3 to 5. These are all Middle to Late Saxon, a period which produced a wide variety of design motifs.
6. Medieval strap-end of plain form.
7. Medieval strap end with trefoil terminal.
8. Another medieval example consisting of two plates fixed to a forked frame with knop terminal.
9. Broken part of a strap-end frame.
10. A more elaborate medieval type, the back plate missing.
11. A circa 14th century strap-end with a hinged pendant.
12. A small strap-end with a 'D' section bar riveted on. This probably located into a locking clasp such as item 32 in the buckles section.
13. Strap end circa 15th - 16th century.

HARNESS AND BELT MOUNTS

14. Celtic terret ring. This is a plain example of common form, but more elaborate ones occasionally turn up with enamelled knobs and decoration in La Tène style.
15. Strap union, Late Iron Age to Roman period.
16. A Late Iron-Age mount in La Tène style. This has a background of red enamel, with inlaid dots of blue and yellow glass.
17. Another terret of Roman date.
18. Roman 2nd -3rd century decorative stud: this ridged design is found on various similar fittings of the period.
19. Mount and phallic pendant. Again probably 3rd century, this style is thought to be from military harness trappings, although such objects also occur on small native sites of the period.
20. Mount of similar form.
21. Mount, possibly a baldrick fitting.
22 and 23. Two more mounts of the same family.
24 to 26. Bar mounts, fixed vertically to straps, and of similar date to the preceding.
27 and 28. Two more types of Roman period mount.
29 and 30. More of these flat section equine mounts would probably be known if they were recognised. They are Anglo-Scandinavian bridle mount fragments in the Ringerike style of the 10th century.
31. A 10th century stud with the vestiges of typical interlace decoration. No fixing obvious, so perhaps fitted in a collar. Easy to dismiss as a button without careful scrutiny.
32. A plain domed mount with 'button' type fixing from a medieval context, but difficult to attribute as a stray find.
33. A medieval mount typified by being made from thin pressed brass sheet and secured by a rivet and small washer where it attached to the strap.
34. A quatrefoil with central rivet hole and four moulded roundels. Circa 14th century.
35. A sexfoil of flat section with a central opening, secured by two small rivets. Circa 14th - 15th century .
36 to 38. Domed studs of similar date.
39. A flat-section quatrefoil with traces of gilding.
40 to 43. Bar mounts from straps, 13th - 15th century.
44. An arched pendant mount. This would have been fixed to a waist belt and accessories such as a purse hung from it.
45. A bar mount for securing an arched pendant mount.

Heraldic harness decorations were popular during the 14th and 15th centuries, and were frequently enamelled. The heraldry is often more decorative than accurate, and the charges do not necessarily denote any allegiance on the part of the owner.

Mounts and Fittings

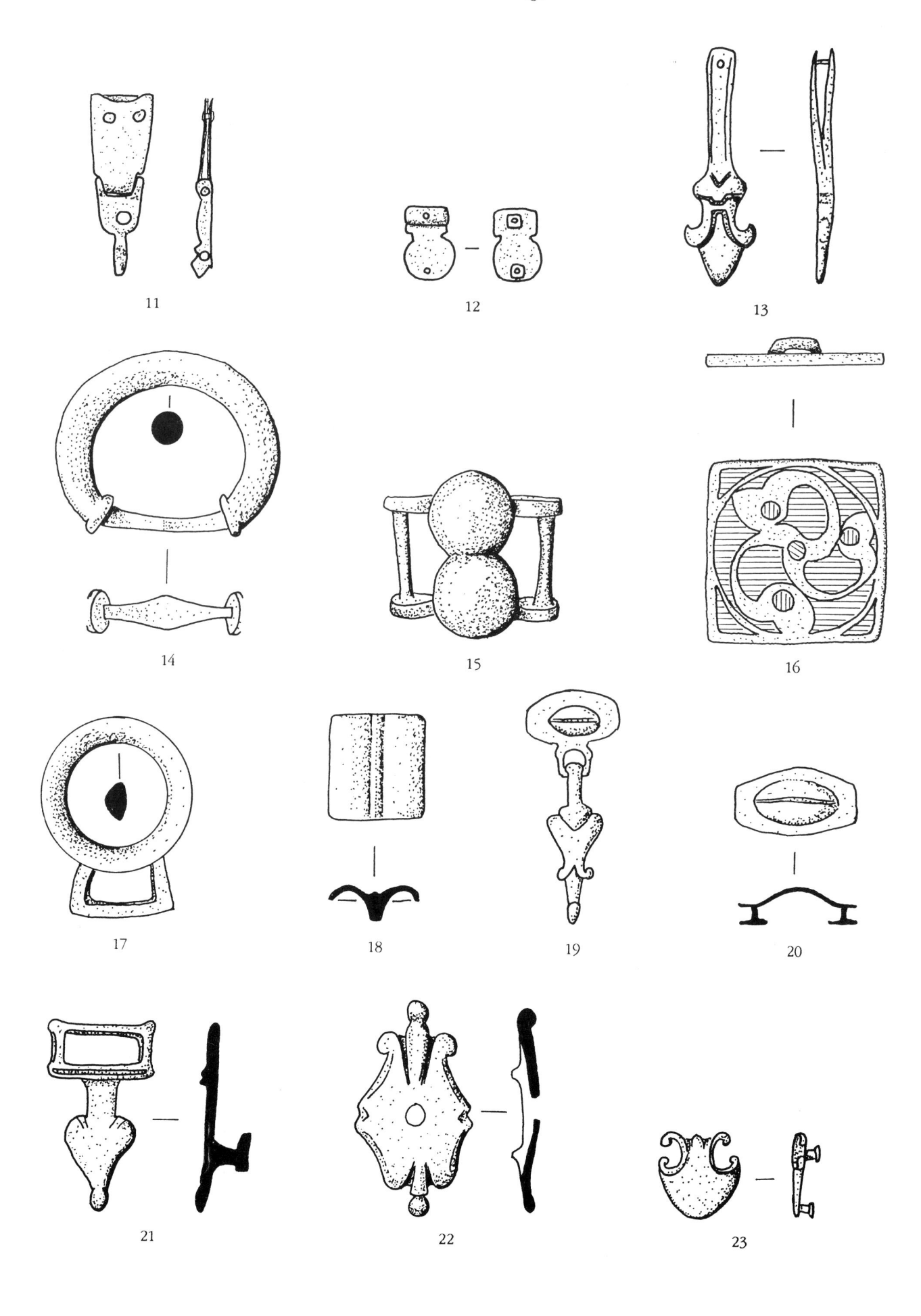

11

12

13

14

15

16

17

18

19

20

21

22

23

Mounts and Fittings

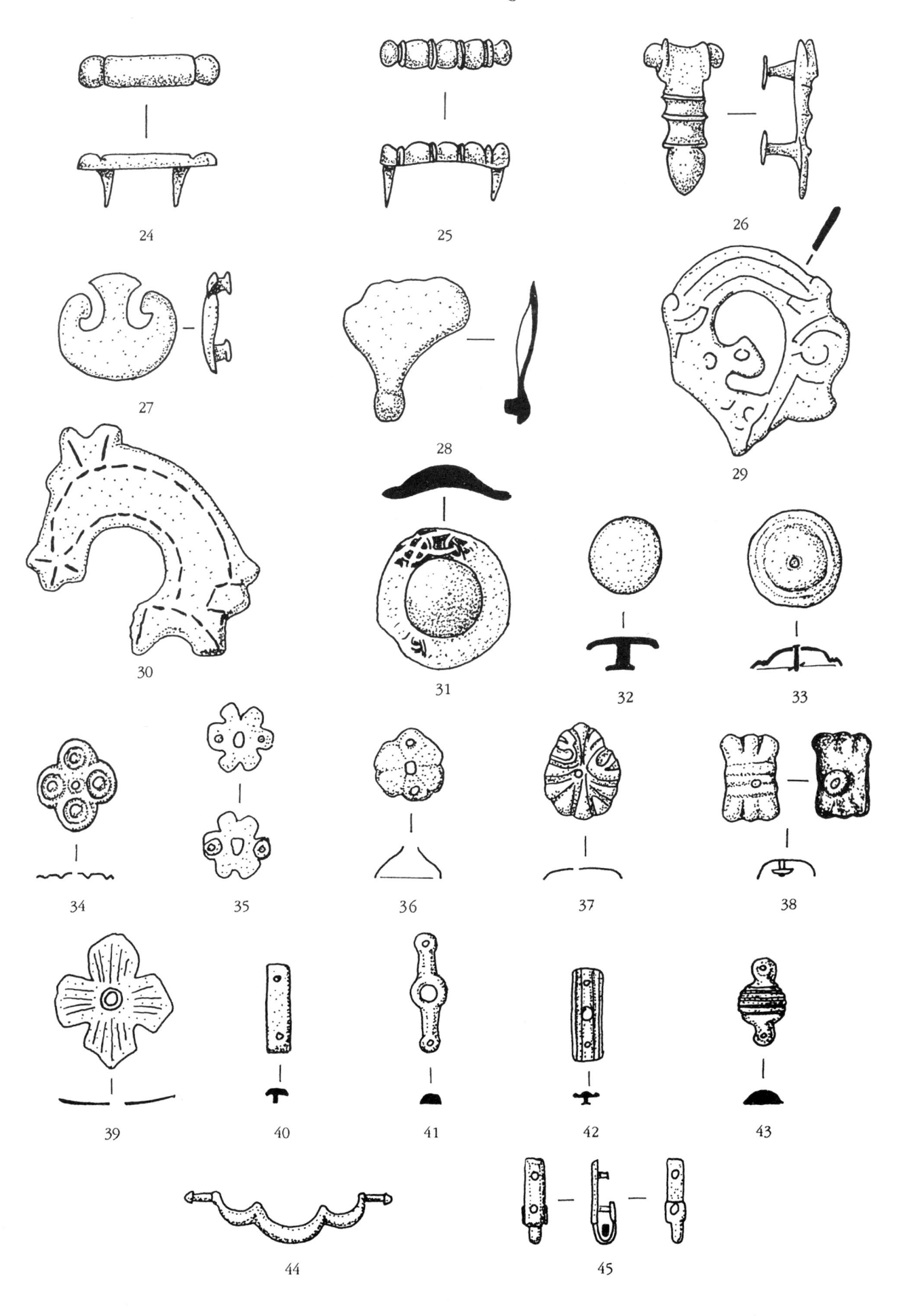

37

Mounts and Fittings

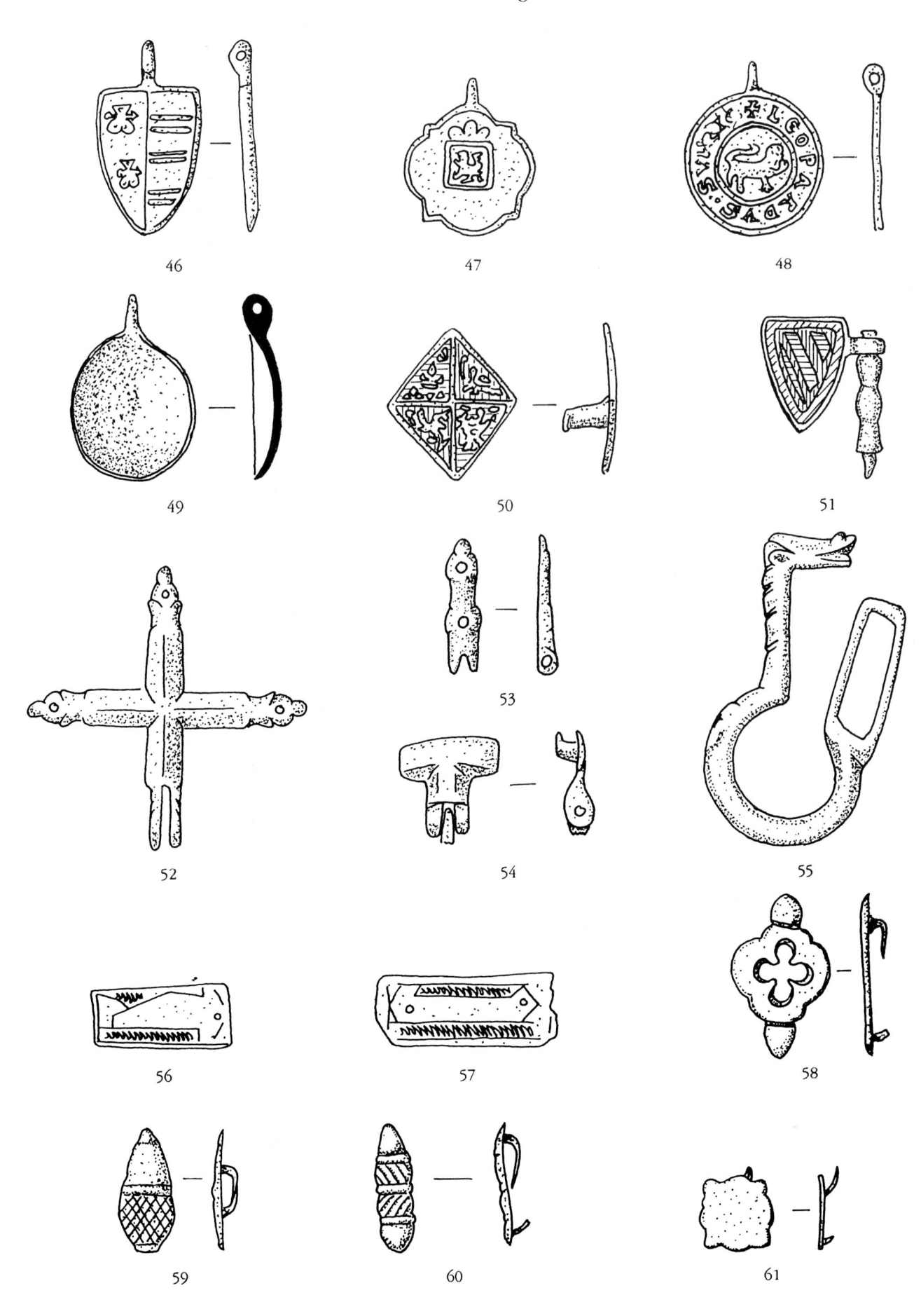

46

47

48

49

50

51

52

53

54

55

56

57

58

59

60

61

Mounts and Fittings

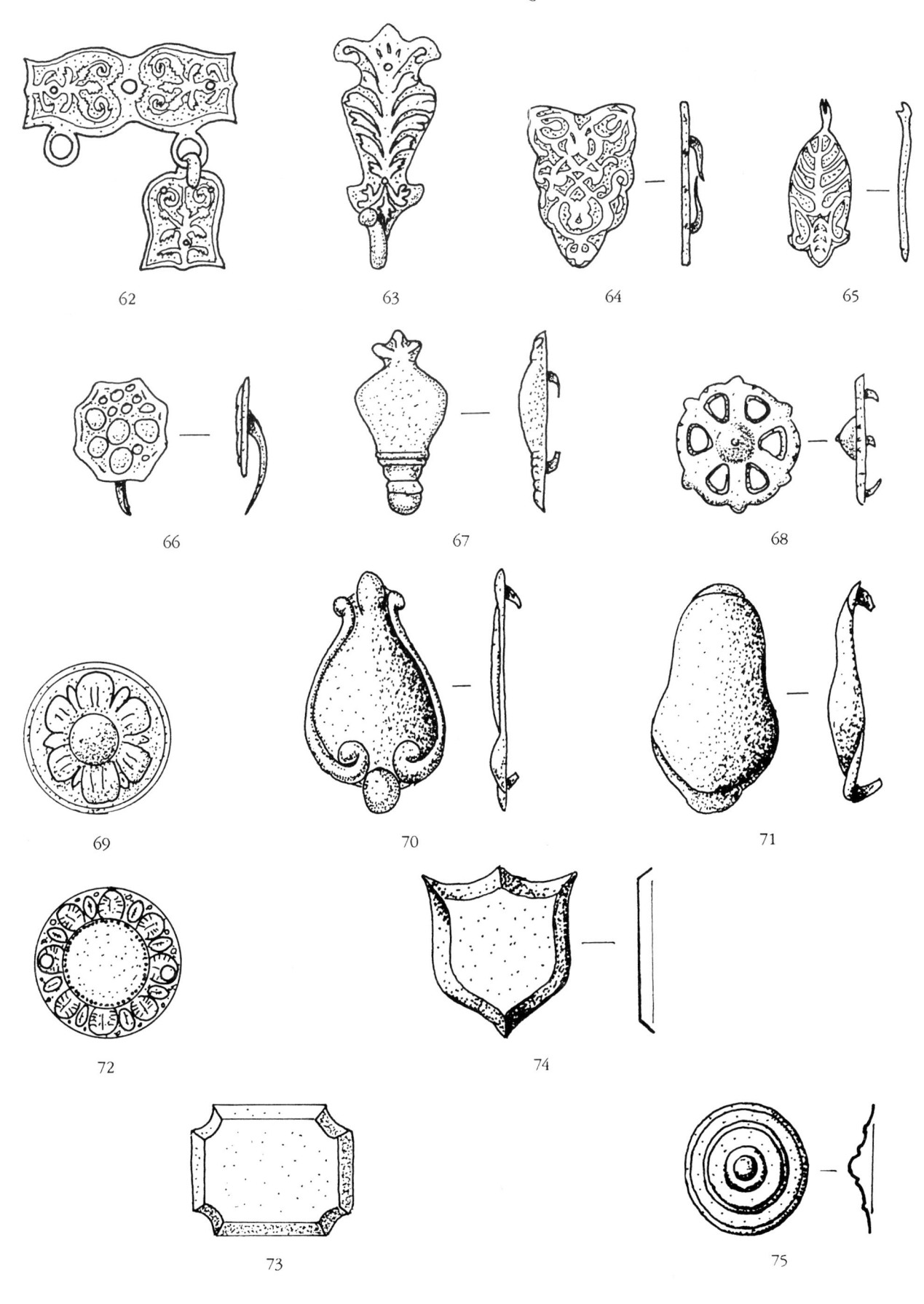

62 63 64 65

66 67 68

69 70 71

72 74

73 75

39

Mounts and Fittings

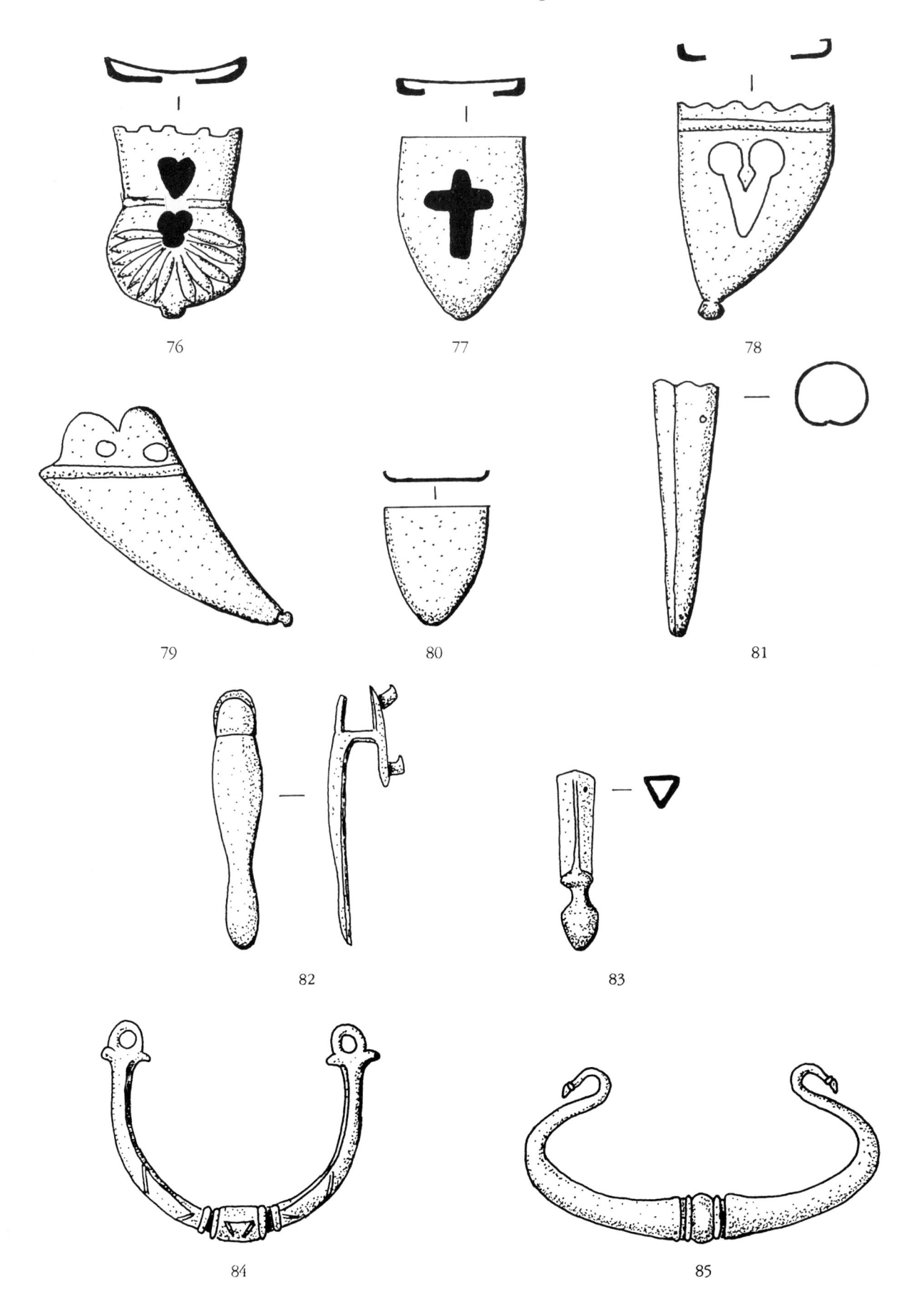

76

77

78

79

80

81

82

83

84

85

40

Mounts and Fittings

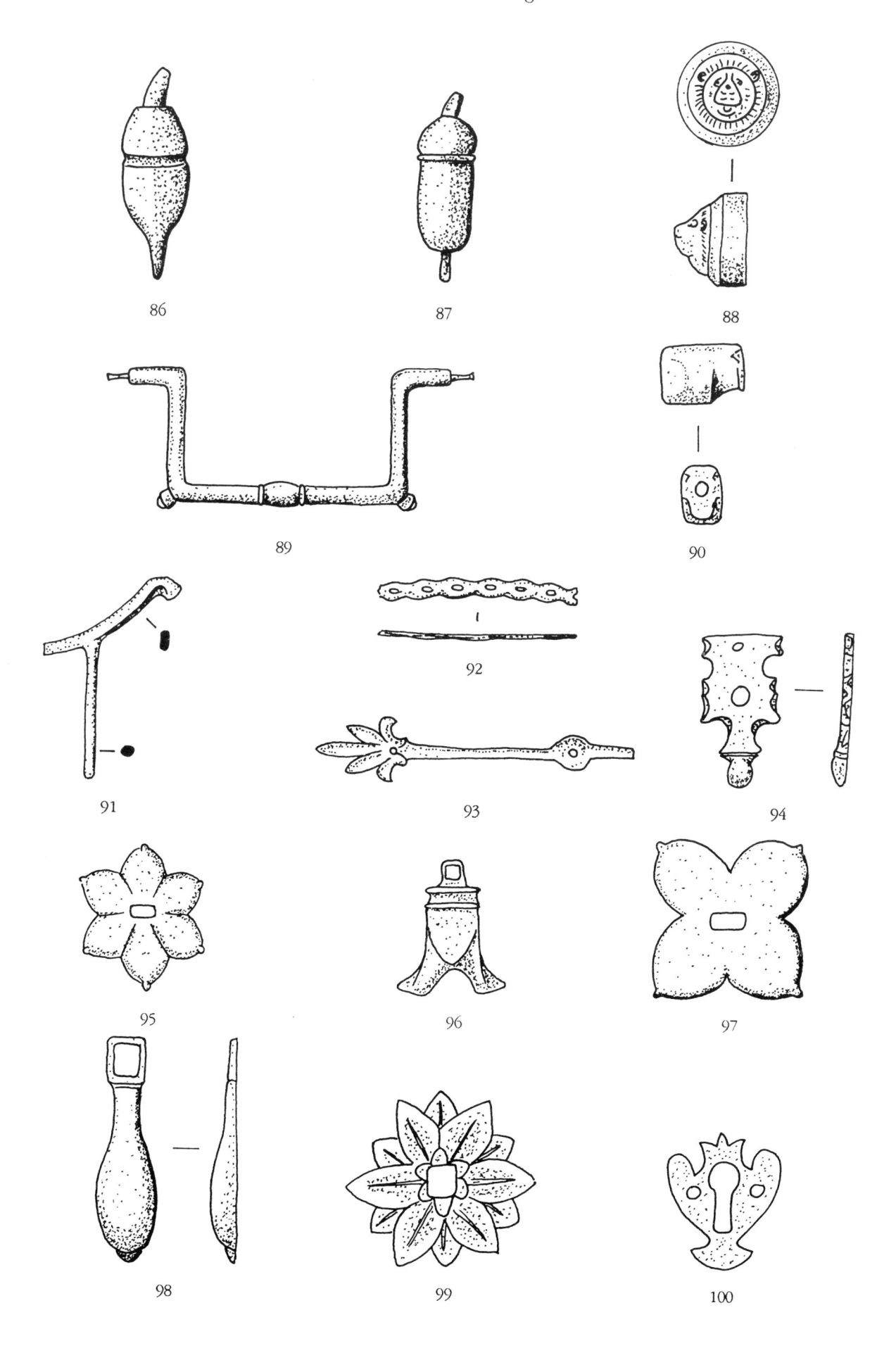

86

87

88

89

90

91

92

93

94

95

96

97

98

99

100

41

Seals and Seal-Boxes

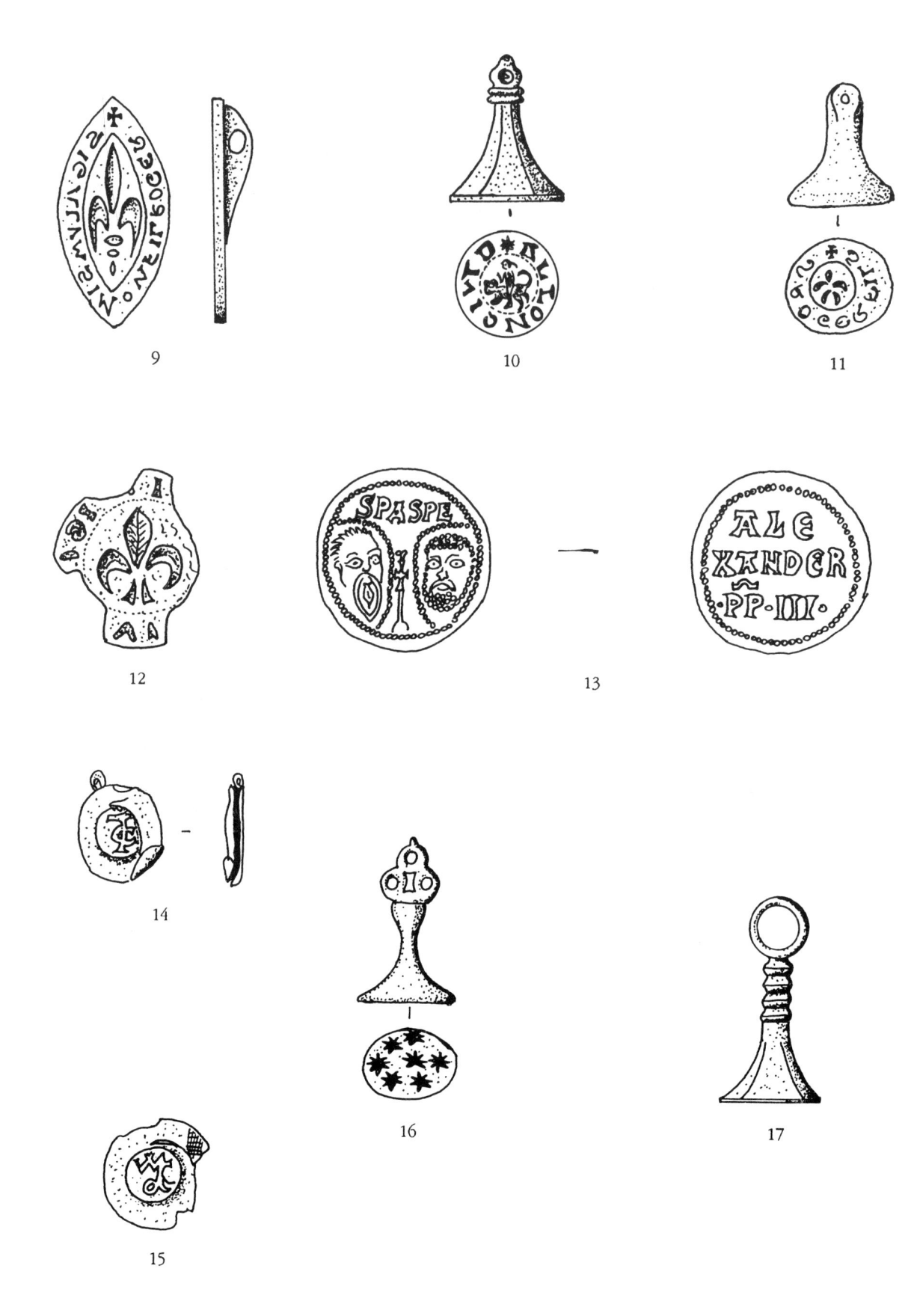

9

10

11

12

13

14

16

17

15

44

Seals and Seal-Boxes

18   19   20

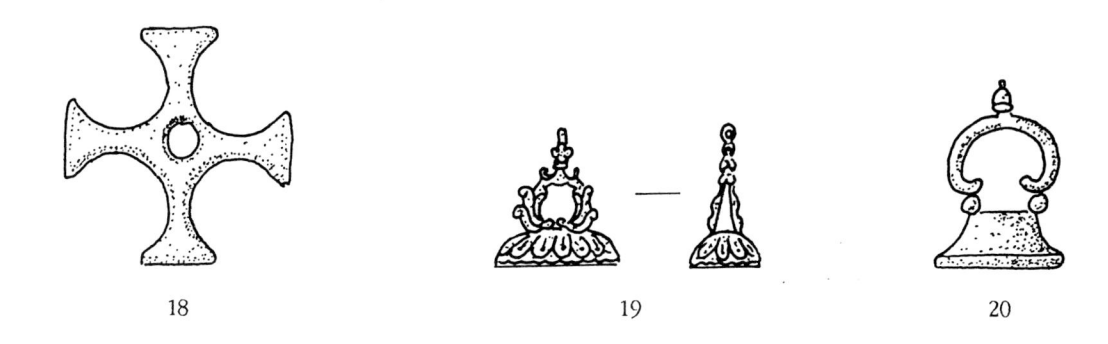

21

SPOONS

The first metal spoons were produced during Roman times and seem to have been limited in use to either ritual functions or the eating of shellfish, for which purpose they were provided with pointed 'rats tail' handles. The idea of sets of cutlery i.e. knife fork and spoon only arose in the 17th century; until then most people used a spoon and general purpose knife, and their fingers.

1. Silver spoon of the Roman period with stepped join between bowl and handle. (Scale 2:3).

2. Another variety with handle and bowl in one piece.

3. Roman period with round bowl, but still with 'rats tail' handle. (Scale 2:3).

4. Fragmentary spoon bowl, typical of a field find.

5. Few specifically Saxon period metal spoons are known, wooden utensils being the norm, and only in the medieval period do they become more general, although still rare finds. Early spoons are characterised by the round 'soup spoon' type of bowl, as in this acorn knop variety of the 14th century. (None of the following to scale).

6. The terminals or knops on spoons follow a number of patterns, and are a guide to dating. This is a detail of a medieval acorn knop.

7. Also medieval, this is a diamond point type.

8. This melon knop was popular in the 16th century.

9. This is a maidenhead spoon of the same period.

10. Apostle spoons became popular in the 16th century, and continue to this day as popular christening gifts. Early ones are identified by style, bowl shape and makers marks. Hall marks only began in the later 16th century.

11. Seal knop spoon of the 17th century. The flat head may be marked with the owner's initials.

12. Slip top spoon of the 17th century, again with the owner's initials.

13. 'Puritan' spoon of the Commonwealth period, other details similar to the slip top.

14. In the later 17th century, the 'trefid' head became popular. Many pewter and brass examples turn up.

15. 'Dog-nose' spoon top, late 17th -early 18th century.

16. Trefid spoon of late 17th century showing owner's initials, makers stamps and bowl back.

17. Top of a silver teaspoon of the Hannoverian period. At this time, spoons were laid back uppermost, and thus the finial was on the inside face of the handle, not the back as is now the case.

18. Shell-back spoon of the same period. The bowl backs were decorated with many similar motifs, such as baskets of flowers etc.

19. Oar pattern spoon handle of later 18th century, a style which continues to the present.

20. Mustard spoons became popular from the later 18th century, the bowls evolving into the round shape used today.

21. (Photograph). Modern base-metal spoons.

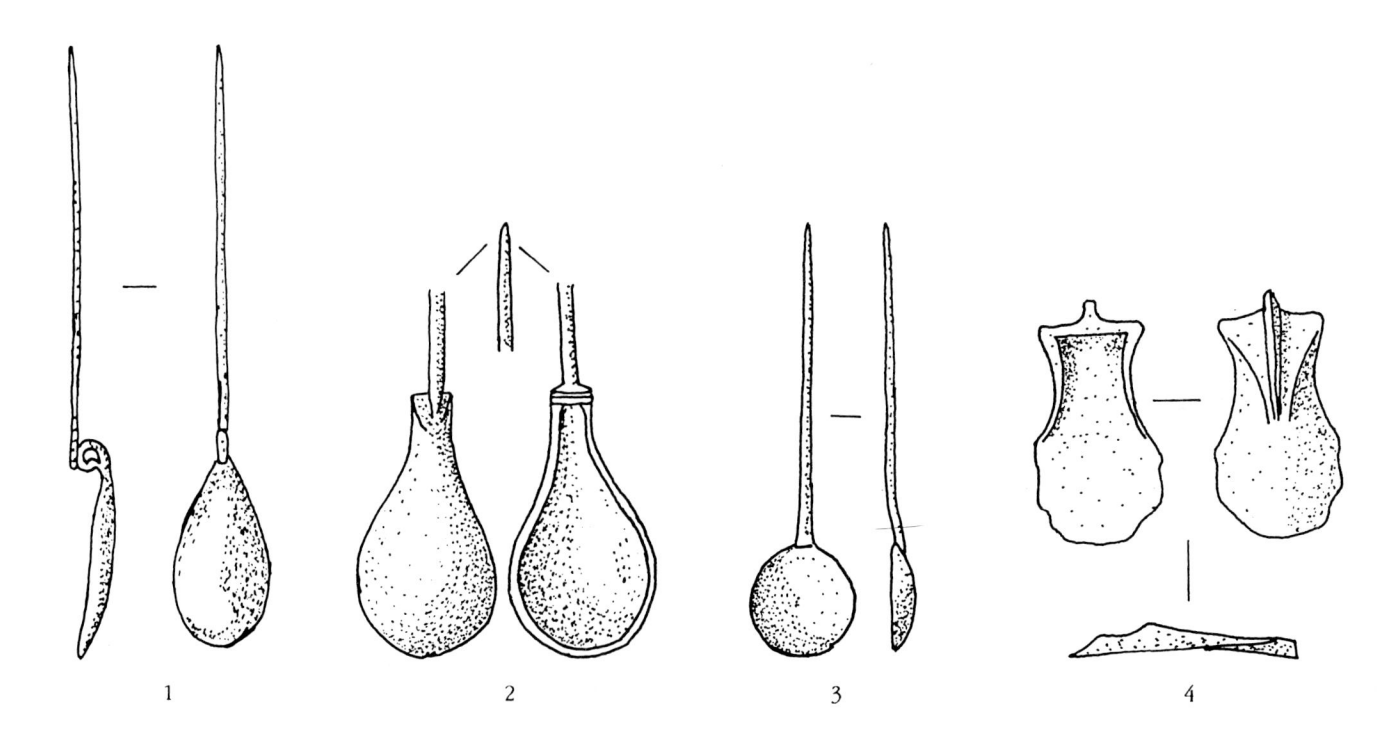

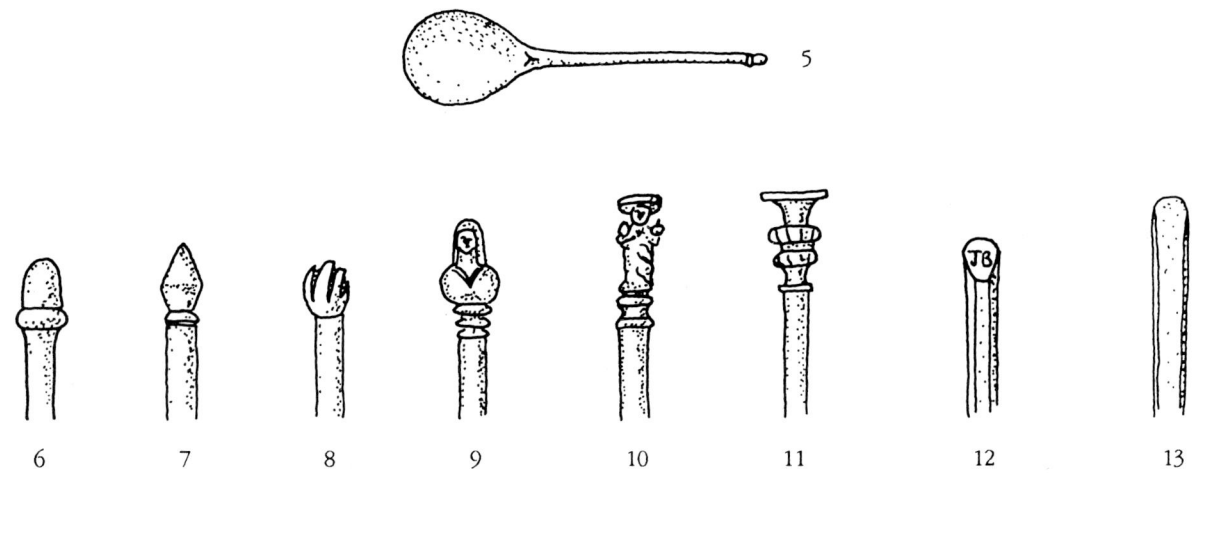

Spoons

5

6 7 8 9 10 11 12 13

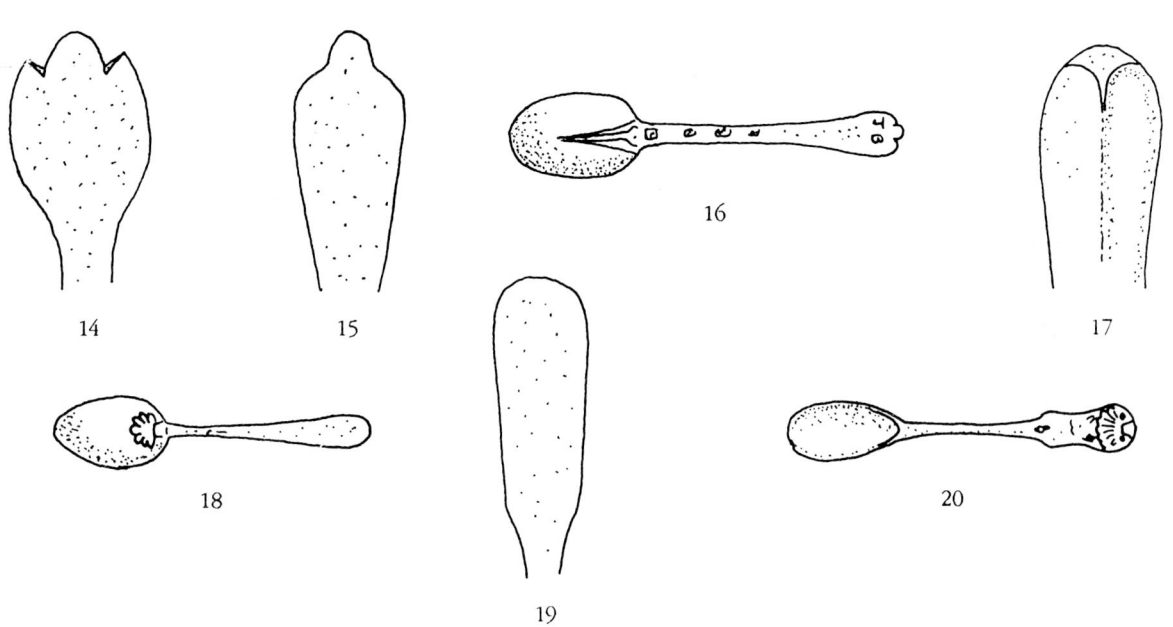

14 15 16 17

18 19 20

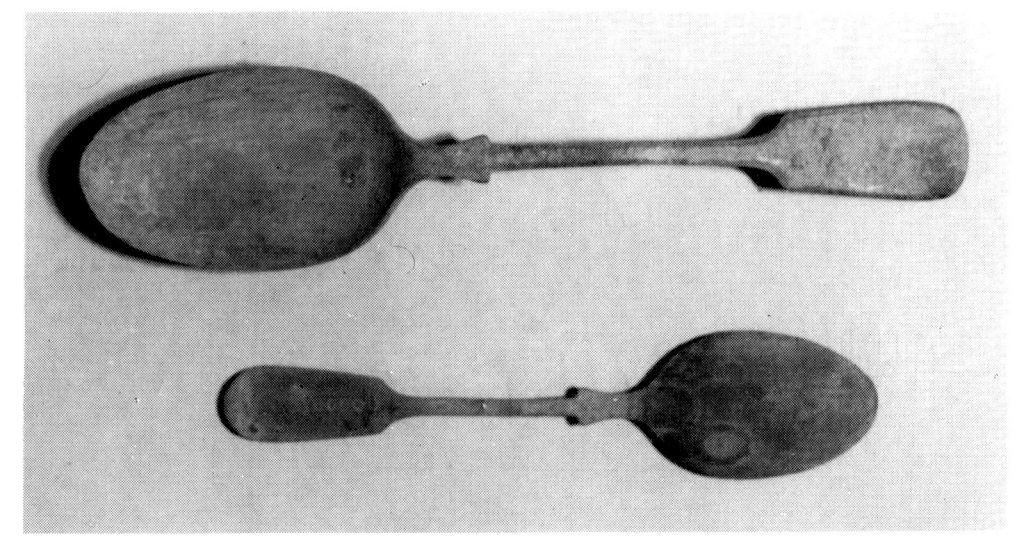

21

47

THIMBLES

Like horseshoes of conventional shape, thimbles are attributed to the Roman period, but with little definite evidence. Those which are described as from Roman contexts are however no different in form to medieval examples, and in the absence of metallurgical analysis an early date must remain speculative. Leather thumb stalls were probably used for sewing, and the thimble may well have originated in the East, either in Byzantium or the Arab world. Because the form is generally basic, precise dating on early examples is only general.

1. Medieval 'beehive' form. These were either cast or hammered from sheet metal. The cast examples often have a small hole at the crown. This example has many fine pits roughly applied in verticle runs.

2. Similar period open top type.

3. Medieval - Tudor period with vertical pits on sides and spiral pits on crown.

4. 16th -17th century example with elongated pits in a spiral on sides and round pits in spiral on crown. This also has a makers mark. The pits by this time were applied mechanically, many examples being imports from Europe, principally Germany.

5. 16th -17th century example of 'beehive' shape with round pits in dense spiral mechanically applied from base to crown.

6. 17th century silver example with scratch engraved initials. The top made separately.

7. 17th century silver example with patterning of blank bands and motto (in this case 'Live to die'). More elaborate examples exist, the portrait of Charles I being a popular theme and thus suggesting a restoration date. Square pits, engraved or stamped are common on these types.

8. 18th century example. Lightly decorated lower part, machine stamped pits to upper body, bolder pits in spiral on crown. Plain crowns also exist.

9. Recent thimble. Well machined with bead rim. Silver and gold examples will be hall-marked or assay stamped. Thimbles became novelty items from the late 19th century, and may bear advertising slogans; some are purely display objects.

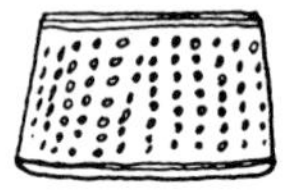

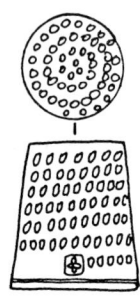

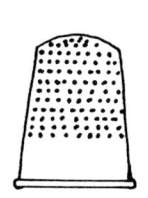

WEIGHTS

As with many things, it is the Romans who are credited with introducing the first weights into Britain. They were used either on pan balances, or on steelyards.

1. Roman period round weight of 10.1 grammes. The only marking is a small 'dimple' in the centre.

2. Another completely plain example weighing 5.6 grammes.

3. Lead steelyard weight with copper-alloy suspension hook. These are common finds on Roman sites, but far rarer are bronze examples, often cast in the form of a bust, and distinguished from pure sculpture by the fact that they have a suspension loop and are usually lead filled.

4. Another variety, this time with an iron suspension attachment.

   Weights were used in the Saxon period but are difficult to date. Some Viking lead weights incorporated Celtic motifs cut from looted metalwork taken from Ireland.

5. Medieval steelyard weight, lead-filled copper alloy. (Scale 2:3).

6. Medieval lead weight, a simple lead disc with a plain raised shield design. Numerous lead discs and odd cubes of lead were used as unofficial weights, and date from medieval times until the 19th century; most are impossible to date with any accuracy.

7. A round weight of the Tudor period, a plain disc of 27.15 grammes stamped with a crowned 'h'. (Scale 2:3).

8. A round lead weight of Elizabeth I. (Scale 2:3).

9. Copper alloy circular weights adopted a standard form from the 16th century, and usually have a rim and engraved circles. Various symbols were used such as the crowned initials of the monarch, the mark of the Founders' Company, and various other stamps. The stamps for George I to George IV are of the same appearance, but were placed at different positions on the weight during each reign. If the weight was avoirdupois it is stamped 'A', and Troy weights were stamped with a conjoined 'TR'. (Scale 2:3).

10. This is a 'bell'- shaped weight, generally of Georgian or later date. (Scale 1:2).

11. Another class of weight was used to test gold coins for forgery. Early methods involved using a tumbrel, which was a balanced arm upon which the coin to be tested was placed, but by the 15th century this had given way to using a pan balance with specific weights relating to different denomination coins. This weight is for a gold noble, and reflects the design on the coin.

12. Another coin weight, this time for an angel.

13. This is a Tudor period fine sovereign weight (which at that time was valued at 30 shillings).

14. A unite weight of Charles I.

15. This is a half-guinea weight for issues pre-dating 1816, the weight being given in pennyweights and grains.

16. Many foreign coins were accepted at various stages of history, although not always with official approval. This is a weight for a Portuguese four-cruzado; the Spanish real or 'piece of eight' was also popular.

17 and 18. In addition to coin weights, apothecaries used small metal weights for weighing various medicines; most are inscribed with weights such as scruples and grains.

19 (photograph). Unmarked lead weights, common finds, mostly late or post-medieval..

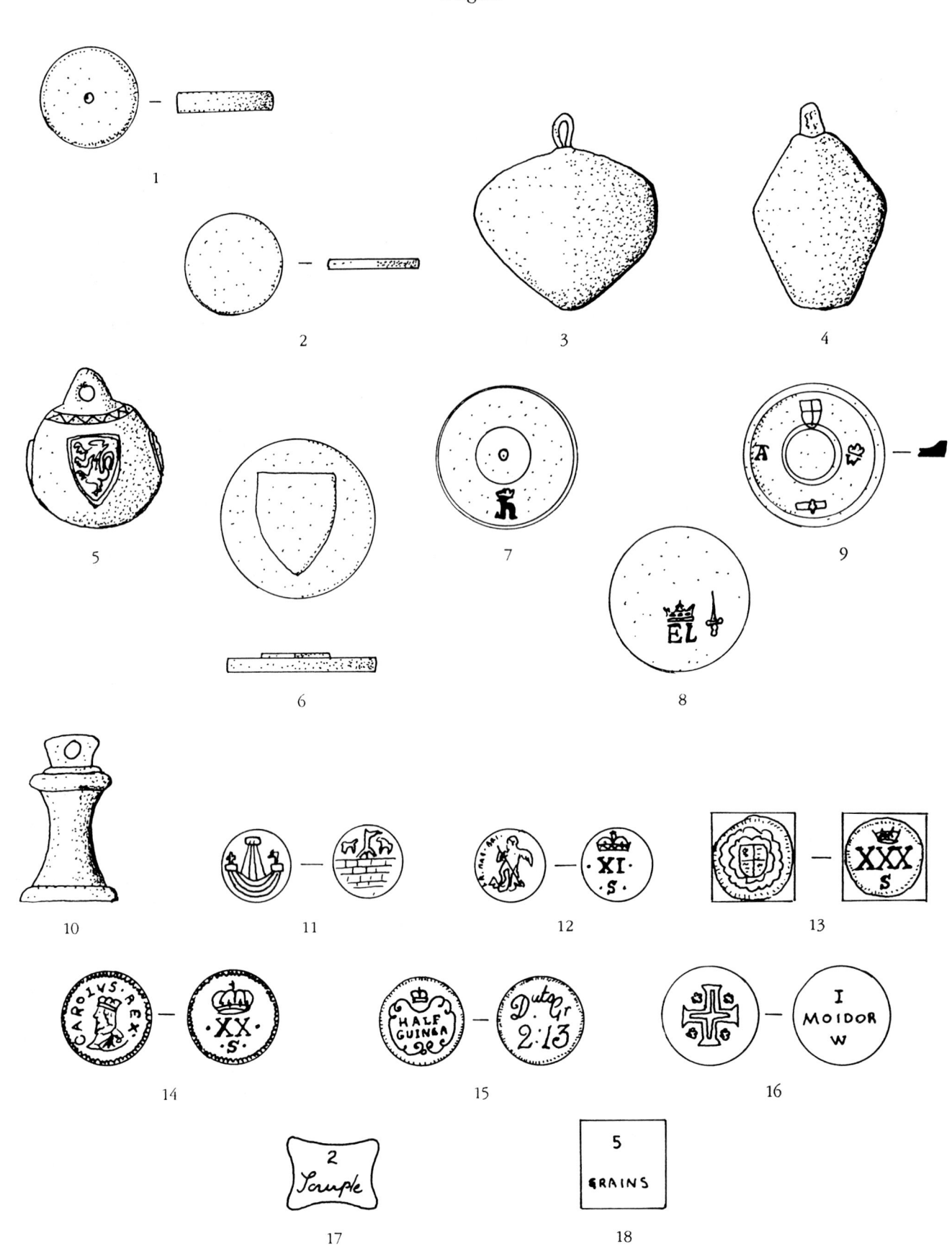

Weights

50

19

MISCELLANEOUS

This section covers a few of the numerous identifiable odds and ends that can be found, but inevitably there are many omissions.

1 to 3. Dating to the Roman period, these are a cosmetic scoop, nail cleaner and tweezers, and although single finds, they once formed sets of implements. These were sometimes suspended from chatelaine brooches.

4. Roman period cosmetic or surgical scoop. Cosmetics often came in long glass bottles of 'test tube' shape, and these implements are presumed to have been used to extract them. Many similar probes were used for surgical purposes. (Scale 1:2).

5. Looking like a screwdriver blade, this is a stylus for writing on wax tablets (see Seal Boxes). The pointed end was for writing, the blunt end for erasing. Usually iron, but bronze ones also exist. (Scale 1:2).

6. Roman period lead pot mend. In the days before 'superglue', storage pots would be mended by drilling a hole on the line of the break, and then running molten lead through which on cooling would hold the pot together. Only the sherd remains can date them, and such finds may also be Saxon or medieval.

7. Roman period lead spindle whorl. Common finds, and again many examples may be post-Roman in date.

8. Roman period domed stud. Tinned bronze, with an iron fixing in mortar. Dome-headed studs are common finds on Roman sites and were presumably used for furniture decoration, just as they were from the 17th century onwards. Occasionally, examples such as this occur and were presumably used for decorative purposes on structures.

9. Roman period embossed copper-alloy sheet. Numerous fragments of bronze sheet occur on Roman period sites, but only when they bear some form of decorative motif can they sometimes be dated. This may have been a decorative strip from a box or suchlike, perhaps based on the designs on Samian Ware.

10. Roman military cuirass hinge. Not a common find, but a distinctive type.

Miscellaneous

11. Roman period model axe. Presumed to be votive offerings, as a number have been found on temple sites.

12 and 13. Any sculpture from the Roman period is scarce, but model animals were popular. Possibly a religious connection, or maybe just toys or ornaments.

14. Small birds were popular, and often have a fixing lug as in this case. Probably decoration from a bronze vessel.

15. Antefix in Celtic native style. Classical style sculpture is rare, but native styles less so. This may have decorated an item of furniture.

16. Clasp-knife or razor handle. A popular theme during the Roman period was this motif of a hound chasing a hare. (Scale 2:3).

17. Cosmetic grinding set. Found as two separate items, but originally used as a set, these are presumed to have been used to powder cosmetics purchased as a solid. They were worn as pendants.

18. Slide pin from a lock. Occasional finds on Roman sites, these formed part of lock assemblies, and slid the bolt to and from the locking position.

19. Lock bolt. From lock mechanism of the Roman period, this engaged the teeth on slide keys.

20. An item peculiar to the pagan Saxon period, these are known as 'girdle hangers', and were worn on female waist-belts. They are presumed to be symbolic of keys, perhaps underlining the female place in the home. (Scale 1:2).

21. A field find, which has been broken.

22. Another popular Saxon period artefact were tweezers, typically with broad ends as with this example. Medieval examples of similar form are also known.

23. The Middle Ages were a time of pilgrimages, such as the one described by Chaucer in his 'Canterbury Tales'. Pilgrims visiting the different shrines around the country, and sometimes overseas, would purchase a badge to be worn on their hat or elsewhere to show they had been. Lead alloy ampullae such as this example were popular, and were probably filled with holy water at the shrine. This example is attributed to Walsingham. (Scale 2:3).

24. Another ampulla, this time with a popular 'shell' motif. Tin was also used but rarely survives on land sites. (Scale 2:3).

25. Lead alloy badges were made in wide variety of forms all relating to the particular attributes of various saints. This is believed to be Thomas Becket from the Canterbury shrine.

26. Another pilgrim badge, the fleur-de-lys symbolising The Virgin.

27. Although similar, many secular badges were also produced, this example depicting the Sun and Moon.

28. These knife handle terminals occur fairly widely, and are tentatively ascribed a medieval date.

29 and 30. Frequently found are legs such as these, often showing evidence of blackening. They are presumed to be the legs of bronze cooking vessels or possibly trivets, which perhaps snapped off fairly frequently due to continual heating and cooling, although why so many occur as stray finds away from domestic sites remains a puzzle.

31. Taps and spouts are occasional finds from the medieval period, and zoomorphic forms were popular.

32. Until the later part of the Middle Ages, spurs were commonly made of iron, copper-alloy gaining popularity in later periods. Complete and undamaged spurs are not common finds, and fragmentary examples are often difficult to date. Spur rowels likewise only follow a very basic chronology, but this iron example with its pronounced spikes is medieval.

33. Another type in copper-alloy, circa 15th - 16th century.

34. Multi-point type, also late medieval - Tudor, but similar to later examples. Small multi-point rowels continue until the present century. Some may be confused with pastry jiggers, but the wheels of these are serrated, not pointed.

35 and 36. A dress item peculiar to the medieval and Tudor periods was the suspended purse, which had either short or long suspension arms. (Not to scale).

37. Suspension loop from a suspended purse.

38. One arm of a purse with inlaid inscription.

39. Another with inlaid decoration.

40. Another common form of bar terminal.

41. Typical field find of part of the lower frame from a purse.

42. Medieval sword pommel. This example is lead-filled copper-alloy. (Scale 1:2).

43. Dagger quillon of medieval date. (Scale 1:2).

44. Dagger quillon of 16th century date. The medieval broadsword went out of fashion and was replaced by the rapier, and it became the practice to fight with a dagger held in the other hand. This quillon is probably from such a dagger. (Scale 2:3).

45. A number of these lead alloy containers are now recorded, and form a specific class of object. One example from the Thames was found containing two dice, and I know of at least two other examples, one from England and one from Belgium, that contained lead tokens dateable to the 15th - 16th centuries. For them to be found with contents intact suggests that they were originally kept within something, perhaps a pouch or box since decayed, and the shape suggests how two might be kept back to back inside a circular container. A gaming use is possible. (Scale 1:2).

46. Small pins were widely used during the 15th - 17th centuries, the heads being formed by crimping the coiled top.

47. Brass lace-ends are difficult to date, but examples such as these occur in medieval and Tudor contexts.

48. Upper part of a silver bodkin. A popular sewing item of the 16th-17th centuries, these large bodkins are often scratch or dot engraved with the owners' initials.

49. Copper-alloy ring. Another specific class of object, generally dateable to the 16th -17th centuries. There are many plain rings of various shapes and sizes which performed different functions, but these rough-cast and often hexagonally-sectioned rings are very common finds. Based on their distribution, being prolific on certain waterfront sites and fair sites as well as occuring widely on arable land, they are likely to be either garment fasteners, or perhaps more probably lashing eyes from tarpaulins and awnings which pre-date ones crimped into the material itself.

50. Toy guns became popular in the 17th century, based on the firearms of the period. They took a small charge and could be fired. (Scale 1:2).

51. Another variety of 17th century toy pistol, this one a typical fragment from arable land.

52. These lead-alloy caps were almost certainly powder measures attached by lanyards through the side-loops to powder flasks or wooden cartridge holders. Mid - late 17th century.

53. Pipe smoking gained great popularity during the 17th century, and tampers were consequently produced. This example is based on a coin of Charles I, and may in fact date from the restoration period.

54. Another 17th - 18th century type incorporated a signet ring. Tampers with decorative mounts were produced up to the 20th century, the bases getting larger in keeping with the increased size of pipe bowls. Political or erotic themes were popular.

55. Jews harp of the 18th - early 19th century. Most medieval examples were of iron, but this later form is fairly common.

56. Watch-keys are frequently found. This is a plain 18th -19th century example which had an iron key bit (now missing). Many elaborate specimens turn up.

57. Another variety of winding key.

58. (Photograph). Many 19th and 20th century badges turn up, of which these are a typical selection.

59. (Photograph). Military badges from the period of the two World Wars.

60. (Photograph) Many agricultural implement fittings occur. These are from cutter bars of 19th -20th century date.

61. (Photograph). A ploughshare of similar date.

62. (Photograph). Plough-share in position on equipment.

Miscellaneous

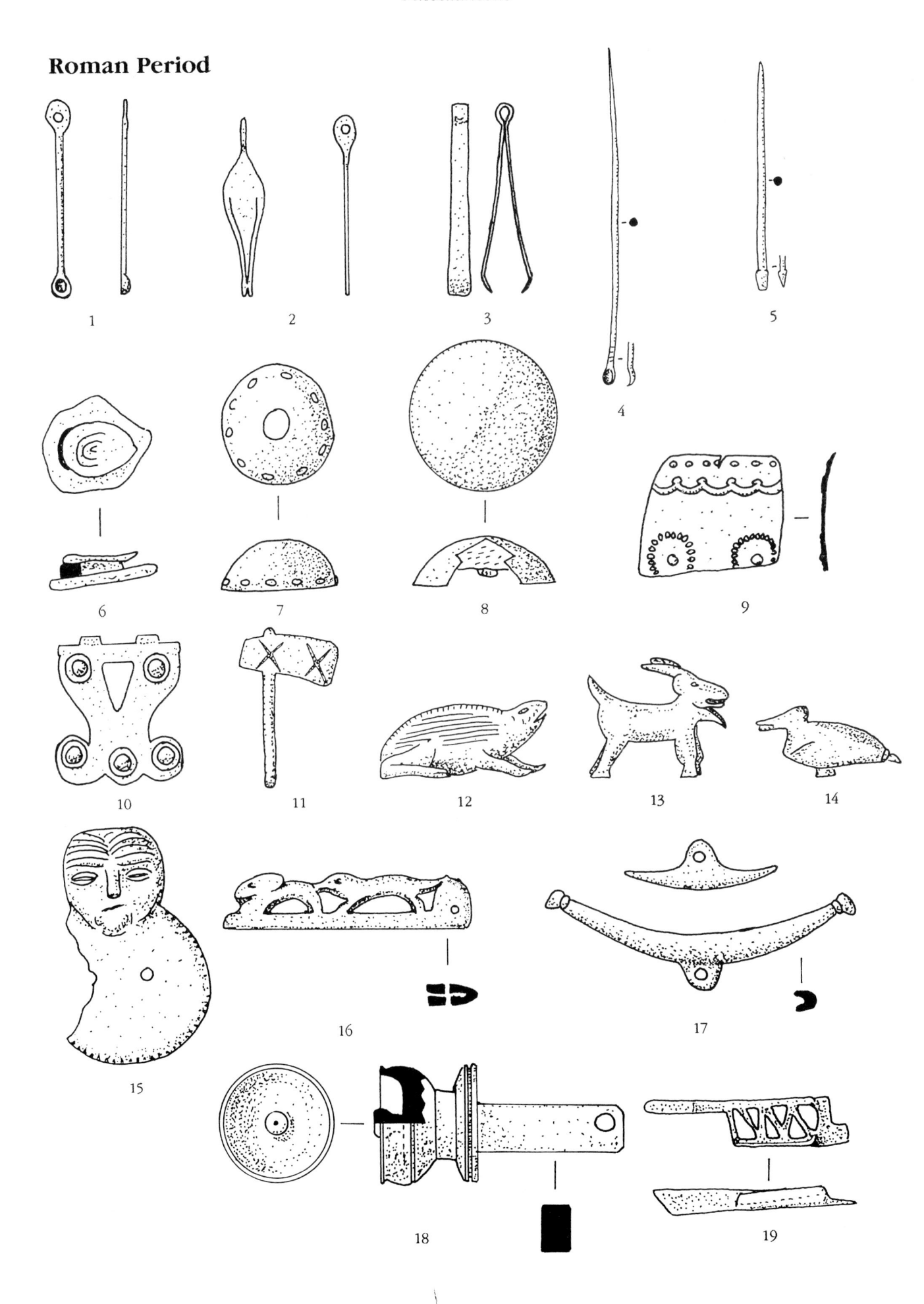

Roman Period

54

Miscellaneous

Saxon and Medieval

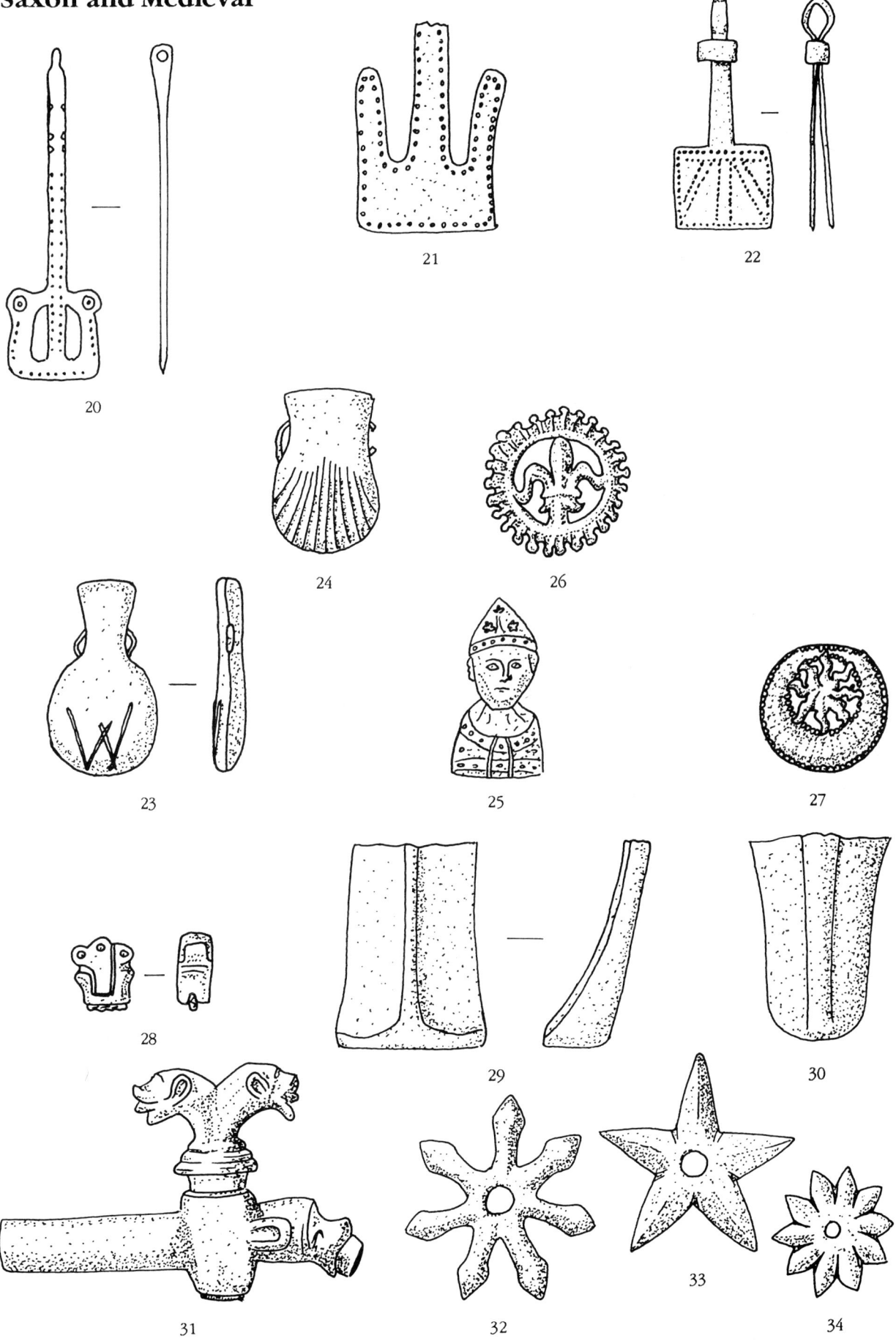

20 21 22

24 26

23 25 27

28 29 30

31 32 33 34

Miscellaneous

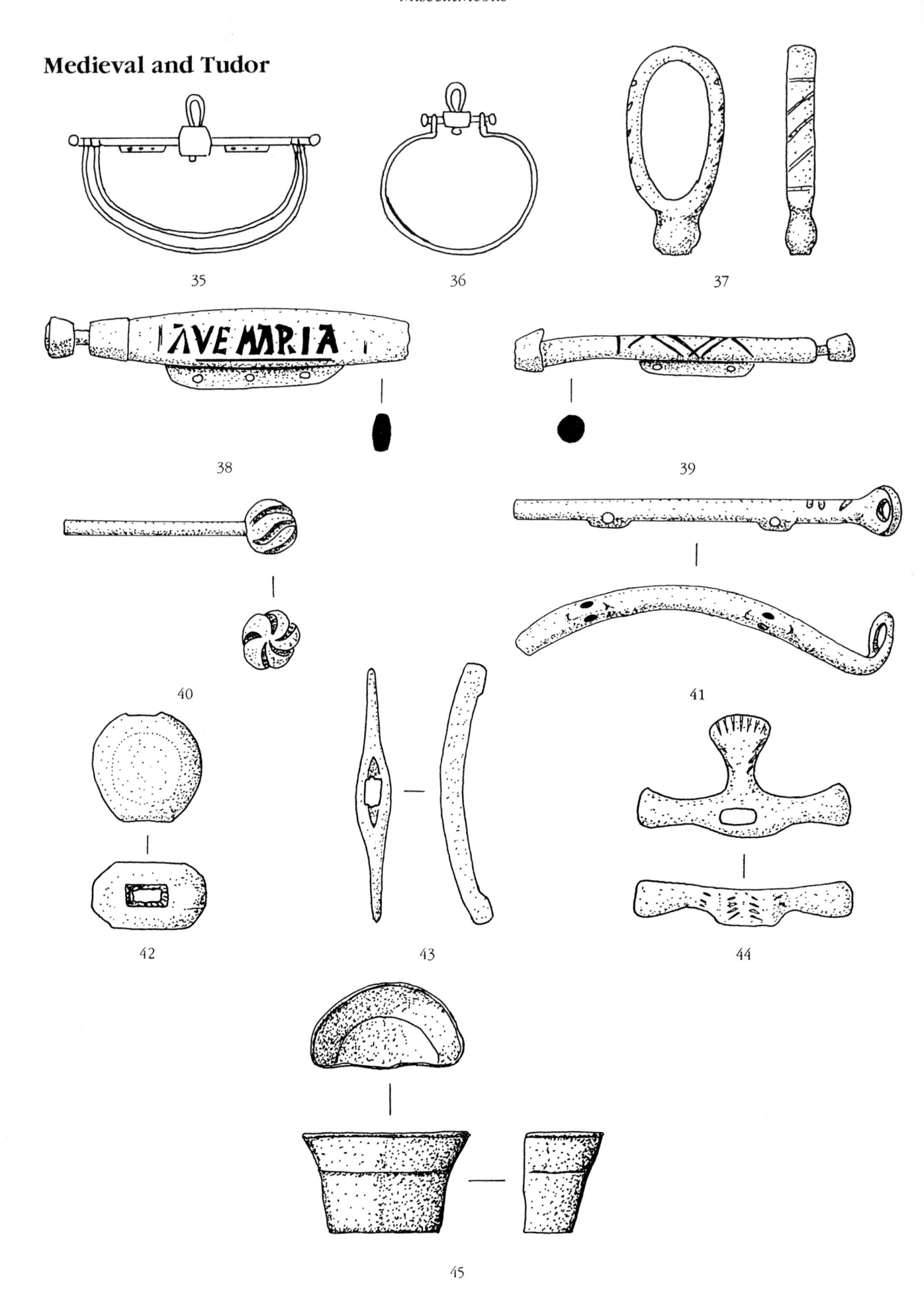

Medieval and Tudor

35

36

37

AVE MARIA

38

39

40

41

42

43

44

45

56

Miscellaneous

Medieval to Recent

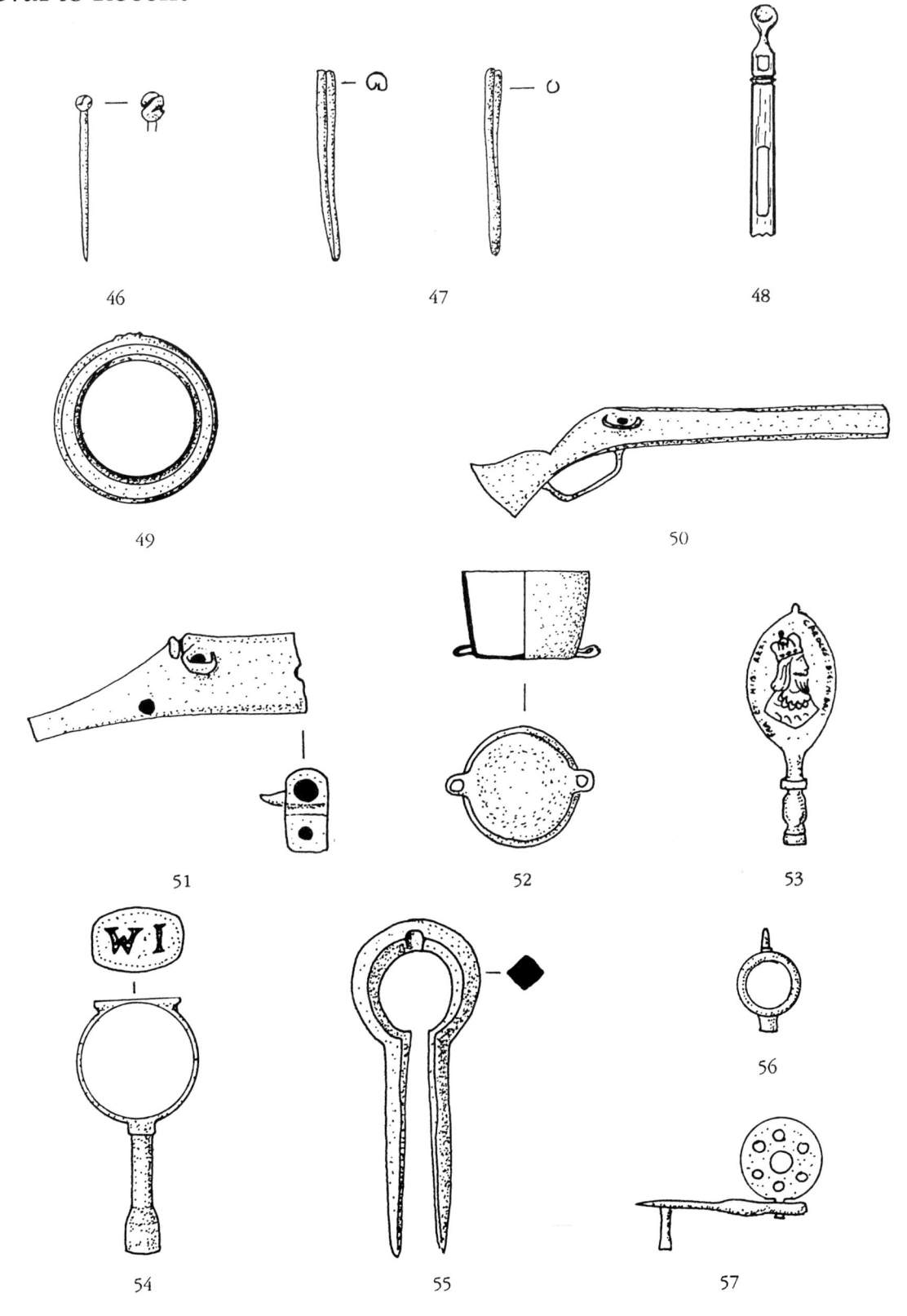

46
47
48
49
50
51
52
53
54
55
56
57

57

Miscellaneous

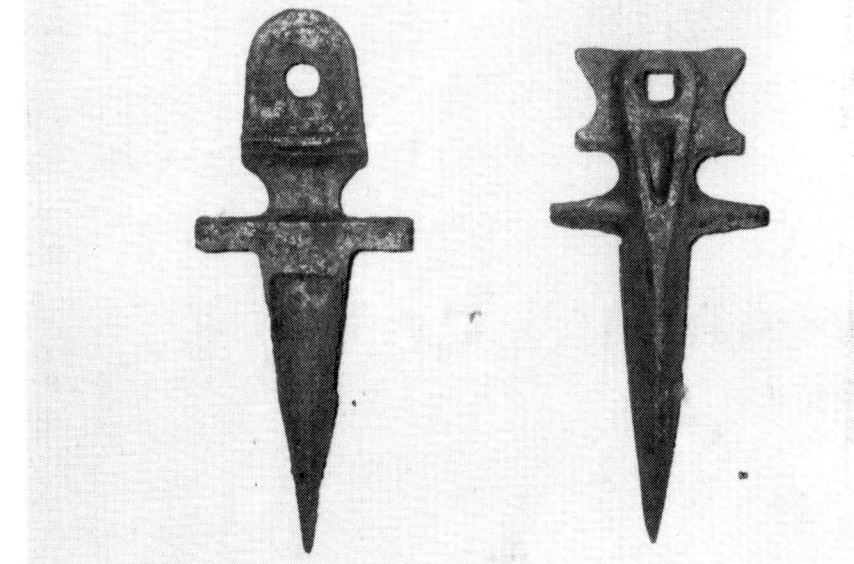

58

59

60

Miscellaneous

61

62

59

SELECT BIBLIOGRAPHY

The following publications will be found useful in seeking a more comprehensive coverage of many items touched on in this book. They have been selected, in the main, for the wealth of illustration which they contain.

Ancient Brooches and Other Artefacts,
R. Hattatt, Oxford, 1989, (reprinted 1992).

Ancient Jewellery. Interpreting the Past,
J. Ogden, London, 1992.

Ancient and Romano-British Brooches,
R. Hattatt, Sherborne, 1982, (reprinted Ipswich 1994).

Apothecaries Weights, N. Biggs, Llanfyllin, 1994.

Ashmolean Museum. A Summary Catalogue of the Anglo-Saxon Collections (non-ferrous metals),
A. MacGregor & E. Bolick, Oxford, 1993.

Badges of the British Army,
F. Wilkinson, Poole, 7th ed. 1987 (reprinted 1992, 1993).

British Coin Weights, P. & B. Withers, Llanfyllin, 1994.

British Museum Guide to Anglo-Saxon Antiquities,
R. A. Smith, London, 1923. (reprinted Ipswich, 1993).

British Museum Guide to the Antiquities of the Bronze Age, revised by R. A. Smith, London 1920.

British Museum Guide to Early Iron Age Antiquities,
R. A. Smith, London, 1925, (reprinted Ipswich, 1994).

British Museum Guide to Mediaeval Antiquities,
O. M. Dalton, London, 1924

British Museum Guide to the Antiquities of Roman Britain, J. W. Brailsford. London, 1951. (2nd edition 1958).

British Rings, 800-1914, C. Oman, London, 1974.

Brooches of Antiquity,
R. Hattatt, Oxford, 1987, (reprinted 1994).

Buttons, G. Squire, London, 1972.

Catalogue of the Finger Rings in the British Museum, Early Christian, Mediaeval and Later,
O. M. Dalton, London, 1912.

Catalogue of the Finger Rings in the British Museum, Greek, Etruscan and Roman,
F. H. Marshall, London, 1907.

Catalogue of Seals in the Public Record Office,
R. H. Ellis, London:
    Personal Seals: Volume I, 1978.
    Personal Seals: Volume II, 1981.
    Monastic Seals: Volume I, 1986.
    (Volume II was promulgated but not published).

Celtic Art, R. & V. Megaw, London, 1989.

The Celts, (marking the Venice exhibition of 1991), various authors, Venice, 1991.

Collecting Shotgun Cartridges,
K. Rutterford, London, 1987.

Collector's Guide to Thimbles,
B. McConnel, New Jersey, U.S.A., 1990.

Domestic Metalwork 1640-1820,
R. Gentle & R. Feild, Woodbridge, 1994.

Dress Accessories c1150-c1450,
G. Egan & F. Pritchard, London, 1991.

English Posies and Posy Rings,
J. Evans, Oxford, 1931.

English Weights. An Illustrated Survey,
N. Biggs, Llanfyllin, 1992 (reprinted 1993).

Finds of Roman Britain,
G. de la Bédoyère, London, 1989.

Finger-Ring Lore, W. Jones, London 1877.

From Viking to Crusader,
various authors, Copenhagen, 1992.

Guide Catalogue of the Bronze Age Collections,
H. N. Savory, Cardiff, 1980.

Guide Catalogue of the Early Iron Age Collections,
H. N. Savory, Cardiff, 1976.

Guide to Harness Decorations,
T. Keegan, 1983, (reprinted 1987 and 1990).

History Beneath Our Feet, B. Read, Braunton, 1988, (2nd revised edition Ipswich due 1995).

Horse Bells, T. Keegan, D. Hughes, C. A. Brock & R. Hawthorne, 2nd edition 1988.

The Hoxne Treasure,
R. Bland & C. Johns, London, 1993.

Iron Age and Roman Brooches,
R. Hattatt, Oxford, 1985. (reprinted 1993).

Lead Cloth Seals and Related Items in the British Museum, G. Egan, London, 1994.

London Museum Medieval Catalogue, J. Ward Perkins, London, 1940, (reprinted 1987 and Ipswich, 1993).

Medieval Pilgrim & Secular Badges,
M. Mitchiner, London, 1986.

The Making of England. Anglo-Saxon Art and Culture AD600-900, L. Webster & J. Backhouse, London, 1991.

Militaria, Arms & Armour, T. Curtis, Galashiels, 1993.

Norwich Households. Medieval and Post-Medieval Finds from Norwich Survey Excavations 1971-78,
S. Margeson, Norwich, 1993.

Pewter. A Celebration of the Craft 1200-1700,
P. R. G. Hornsby, R. Weinstein and R. F. Homer, London, 1989.

Roman Military Equipment,
M. C. Bishop & J. C. N. Coulston, London, 1993.

Saddlers Brasses, R. Hawthorne, 1993.

Salisbury and S. Wilts Museum Catalogue, Salisbury:
    part 1, Arms, Armour, Coins, Horse Pendants, Rings, Spurs, Weights, Textiles, Tiles and Stonework, Saunders & Saunders,1991.
    part 2, Pilgrim Souvenirs & Secular Badges, B. Spencer, 1990.

Thimbles, E. F. Holmes, Dublin, 1970.

Treasures & Trinkets, T. Murdoch, London, 1991.

Victoria and Albert Museum Catalogue of Rings,
C.C. Oman, London, 1930, (reprinted Ipswich, 1993).

The Work of Angels. Masterpieces of Celtic Metalwork, 6th-9th centuries AD,
S. Youngs, London, 1989.

In addition, many useful little booklets covering a wide range of related subjects are published by Shire Publications Ltd in their Archaeology and Albums series.

Not all of the reference books and collectors' titles listed above are still 'in print', but many are and can be obtained from Anglia Publishing. Not only do we publish facsimile reprints of important old books and significant new works in this field, but we also encourage other publishers to keep their relevant titles in print by acting as distributors, thus ensuring the widest possible retail availabiity. We would be pleased to supply you, wherever possible, or advise you of your nearest stockist. An up to date list of available titles from many publishers is available on request. Our full address appears on the title page.